THE CREATIVE POWER OF IMAGERY

*'Imagination is more important
than knowledge'*
— Albert Einstein

Dr Ian Gawler, *OAM, BVSc.*

The inner world of Meditation and Imagery has been a major focus of Ian Gawler's life for over twenty years. As a cancer patient who was fortunate to experience a remarkable recovery, Ian was involved in the pioneering days when these techniques were developed and first applied to healing in the western world. Over the years Ian has learnt from many recognized Masters, both from traditional backgrounds and in the rapidly developing medical field of Psychoneuroimmunology or Mind/Body Medicine. He now lectures around the world on these themes.

More importantly, what Dr Gawler has to offer is the accumulated experience and wisdom of the many thousands of people he has worked with. Since 1981 when he began to conduct active, solution-based support groups for other people affected by cancer, his work has expanded into a dual role. One aspect is the focus on healing, the other on health and wellbeing. So Dr Gawler has developed many techniques for stress management and disease prevention and there he has a major interest in helping people to fulfil their potentials. This has led to techniques for fulfilling excellence in sport and work. Ian has also helped many people in their quest for peace of mind and enlightenment.

Dr Gawler is the author of three bestsellers as well as the editor of five books on Mind/Body Medicine. He is Therapeutic Director of The Gawler Foundation which employs thirty people and conducts groups and residential programs amidst the peace and tranquillity of the Yarra Valley in Victoria, Australia.

The Creative Power of
Imagery

A practical guide to the workings of your mind

Dr Ian Gawler
OAM, BVSc

MICHELLE ANDERSON PUBLISHING
MELBOURNE

By the same author (all published by Michelle Anderson Publishing):
YOU CAN CONQUER CANCER
PEACE OF MIND
MEDITATION – PURE & SIMPLE

Edited by Ian Gawler (all published by The Gawler Foundation):
NEW CANCER PERSPECTIVES
INSPIRING PEOPLE
MIND, IMMUNITY AND HEALTH
THE MIND, BODY CONNECTION
SCIENCE, PASSION & HUMOUR

Published by Michelle Anderson Publishing Pty Ltd
PO Box 6032, Chapel Street North, South Yarra 3101
Tel: 9826 9028
Fax: 9826 8552
email - mapubl@bigpond.net.au
website: www.michelleandersonpublishing.com

© IAN GAWLER 1997

Reprinted 2004

Cover photograph: Michelle Anderson
Photograph of Author: Derek Hughes
Cover design: Deborah Snibson, The Modern Art
    Production Group, Melbourne, Victoria

Typeset by: Schuurman Computer Service,
33 Don Road Healesville Vic

Printed by: McPherson's Printing Group, Maryborough, Victoria

Cataloguing-in-publication data

Gawler, Ian, 1950–
The creative power of imagery

Bibliography.

ISBN 0 85572 281 9

1. Mind and body.   2. Imagery (Psychology).
3. Visualization.   I. Title.

153.32

Contents

Foreword and Gratitude

Imagery is a wonderful inner technique that has transformed many lives. Its dramatic benefits are to be seen in sport, business, relationships, healing and in personal development and spiritual practice.

We live in a world of images. Images are thrust at us via the media and advertising. We think in images, fantasize in images; plan and remember by using images. It seems clear that successful people use Imagery naturally and effectively. We all do to some extent, but most have little training in how to use this key to the active part of our mind. This book then, is offered as a user's guide to the inner workings of your mind.

This book is the product of the wide range of experiences I have had over the years using Imagery myself and helping others with it. Imagery is dynamic, powerful, fun; challenging and transformative. It also has the capacity to be a double edged sword. While overwhelmingly my experiences with Imagery have been positive, this is a technique that certainly can be destructive.

So with this book I have aimed to detail the wide range of Imagery techniques that I have used regularly and therefore can share from direct experience. These techniques range across the breadth and depth of life — from sport to business, from relationships to health, healing and peace of mind.

Much of my work has involved participating in people's lives after they have been confronted by life-threatening illness. The intensity of these situations has brought a sharp focus to this inner work. The intensity has cut through any waftiness and led to the heart of the matter — what to do, what works, how to deal with any complications. This aspect of my work has been a great testing ground for the development of these techniques.

In a way, it has been a delight to be able also to work with so many well people. A lot more has been learnt from working closely with sporting and business people, those seeking more peace in their lives, and those who are really yearning for a direct and profound spiritual experience.

The point is that the techniques in this book are based in life. They are based on real life experiences and are well tested. While Imagery has its pitfalls, I hope to have alluded to these clearly through the text. The emphasis is on what does work and how you can proceed into your own direct experience of the wonderfully creative realm of Imagery.

This is dynamic work so I am happy to receive correspondence on your experiences. Also at The Gawler Foundation I have colleagues who can help if you find that difficulties arise and you need help. The best safety net to offset any problems with Imagery is to practise Meditation on a regular basis. This will provide a balance and a calm grounding for the more dynamic inner work of Imagery.

When it comes to practising the many exercises in this book, you will find that some are easy to do having read the directions. Others are more complex and it can be helpful to listen to them so that you are free to focus on the inner work. You may therefore, find it helpful to use the text as a basis for recording your own tapes. I have recorded the key Imagery exercises and also there is a list of tapes available to help you with your meditation practise. The details are at the back of the book.

I would like to thank Derek Hughes for his photography and kind, generous spirit; Deb Snibson has done a great job with the cover and also many thanks to Robbie Schuurman who is an exceptional typesetter and a wonderful help in all aspects of the writing. Thanks too to my publisher Michelle Anderson who has done a wonderful job putting it all together.

A final, heartfelt thanks to all those who have shared their stories in this book. I have changed everyone's names except for Debbie Flintoff-King. Debbie's story is very much in the public domain and I thank her for sharing it again in this forum.

I trust that any merit that flows from this book flows to those wonderful people who I have taught and who have taught me.

Ian Gawler

CHAPTER 1

INTRODUCTION

The pitfalls and the possibilities

When I was eleven, I fell in love with high jumping. It was introduced to me by a rather fierce sports master; predictable in his fierceness, uncompromising in demanding the best of his students, and exquisitely subtle in giving praise indifferently. In short, this teacher scared the hell out of me, recognized a talent I had and demanded I discipline myself to develop it. After the first few terror-filled lessons, where I struggled to understand what was being taught, I soon felt the thrill of flying through the air effectively. High jumping became a passion. I jumped at school, my father built me uprights and landing bags and I jumped at home. It became a delight, an exuberant expression of youthful joy and vigour.

Then an extraordinary event occurred. When I was twelve, I was selected to represent my school at the Inter-School Athletics Carnival. The memory of the day stays clear in my mind. Large flat oval, spreading out into just as flat parklands, with only the occasional tree. Grass somewhat dried by the warm summer; a few greener patches from watering. A small crowd of parents and other competitors gathered around as the bar was steadily raised. A clear blue sky, clear as could be. Radiant in my memory. The feeling of relief, hope and thrill as each of the other boys dropped out. Then only me left, the existing record jumped and the bar continuing to rise. The feeling is new, magical. Nothing like this has happened before. It seems so easy, almost effortless. The memory is of almost being in a dream at the time of each jump. On I go, eventually jumping two inches over my head before I finally begin to think *'this is too high for me'* and I miss the next height.

Then the extraordinary. The local paper covers the competition and runs a headline

   'Schoolboy jumps 2"over his head.'

My passion for highjumping extends to athletics in general, and as I grow older I get into the habit of training regularly and experimenting with all the athletic events. It turns out that I am reasonable at most, but not exceptional at any. So I become a natural for the decathlon, which combines 10 athletic events over two days. This collective event becomes a major focus of my life.

But here is the extraordinary bit. In my late teens and early twenties, I was fortunate to train under an exceptional coach with top athletes, including many Olympians. High jumping remained my favourite, although I performed better at some of the other events. It came to puzzle me that despite all the training, the coaching, the weight lifting, the experience, the wonderful peers, I never jumped higher than 6'4". In fact I became quite reliable. I jumped that height, my maximum, at almost every important competition. Why never higher? What a puzzle.

It was not until after I developed cancer, had my right leg amputated and learnt something of Imagery that I made the connection: *Schoolboy jumps 2" over his head!* I had grown 6'2" tall. I nearly always jumped 6'4" — 2" *over his head!*

Reflecting back to school days, each year I had jumped well, but, you can guess it — just 2" over my height; never more, never less! It seems that I had formed an image of myself being able to jump that 2" over my head and that it stayed with me throughout my athletic career. Anything more was too high for me!

Many years later I was approached by Debbie Flintoff-King for help in her preparation for the 400 m hurdles before the

Seoul Olympics in 1988. Debbie was hoping to learn how to relax and to sleep better before competitions. Also she was concerned that Imagery, or Inner Rehearsal, seemed to escape her. Ranked number two in the world at that time, she was worried that she was missing out on a part of the inner game that might make all the difference for her.

Knowing that I had been a 400 m hurdler and that now I had a deep interest in Meditation, Relaxation techniques and Imagery, Debbie approached me for help. She had been given the impression that Imagery was important (true!) and that it had to be done in a particular way (not true! It has to be done in a way that works for the particular individual who is using it!). Debbie had found that she could not easily create a mental image of herself as if she was actually in her body and running a race. She could see herself running and hurdling as if on a video clip, but even then only vaguely. In talking with her, it was obvious that the first half of her 400 m race was so strong and that she was so confident of it that it needed no attention. Whatever Debbie was doing there, it was working exceptionally well. Where there was a problem was that it was almost as if she went to sleep (relatively) on the second bend, getting little real drive as she almost cruised around the corner, before switching on again and coming home very powerfully. Debbie had an amazing finish.

So we realized that she needed a trigger to focus her efforts on the second bend. What she needed was to actually switch ON at the start of the second bend. She also needed to improve her hurdling style around the bend so that she could alternate her leading leg. We began to work on this using Imagery that Debbie found effective. For her it was done more with words and feelings. While Debbie worked in her mind on the hurdling technique, most of it was done by talking it through, feeling the surge of power, feeling coming home strongly and then feeling the delight of the end result — being up on the dais as she was presented with the gold medal.

In reality, the race final was one of the most extraordinary in Olympic history. Debbie ran hard, smooth and fast for the first two hundred metres. She switched on around the bend and drove on as she alternated her leading leg and hurdled strongly. Yet coming into the home straight she was placed only fourth and looked to many outside observers to be in a hopeless position. Yet Debbie knew the power of her finish; she had an image of herself finishing hard and fast and she had a strong image of her victory. With each hurdle she drew closer. Over the last, it was just the Russian athlete Ledovskaia who was in front. As the finishing line drew closer the Russian appeared to slow, Debbie pushed on tenaciously. A lunge at the line and who had won? The Russian was announced first by the commentators, then indecision, then the replay and the official announcement. Debbie had won by the smallest of margins — one hundredth of a second!

Clearly many things contributed to that memorable win — the hours and hours of unrelenting training, her husband Phil's support and coaching, the sad death of her sister in an asthma attack just days before the race, Debbie's new-found ability to relax, and her motivation to dedicate her race to her sister's memory. Then of course there was her own intense desire to win. But also that inner image of winning, that belief created within herself and held to so clearly, that practice with inner rehearsal. All of this inner work played a major part in what kept her in the race when, despite her best ever first 300 metres, she found herself coming into the straight so far behind in the race of her life. She believed it was possible, she had a clear image of winning and she pushed on to do just that in Olympic record time!

So in athletics, I personally experienced the limitations imposed by inner images, while I shared in the thrill of them working positively.

Now the truth is that we live in a world of images. Images flood the world around us, being projected by television, film, photography and life itself. Everything we experience, everything that registers with our senses, forms an image that is taken in to be stored in our memory. Internally we think using images, remember using images, create using images. Our whole life is affected dramatically by the images that come to us or that we produce ourselves. Images have a major impact on health, healing and wellbeing.

As part of the inner work I did to overcome my cancer more than twenty years ago, I used an active form of Creative Imagery. With my veterinary background, I was aware that there were cells called osteoblasts whose job was to remodel bone. For example, if you were to fracture a bone, your body would first form a large callus around the break, then lay down new bone on this framework. For a while the repaired bone would appear on X-ray to have a solid lump of bone wrapped around the old fracture site. However, with more time, the osteoblasts would steadily nibble away the excess bone, remodelling the area so that eventually it would look just as before — totally healed, even a little stronger now at the place where the break had occurred.

My cancer was an osteogenic sarcoma, which meant that wherever it spread it grew new bone! So I began to imagine cells which I labelled as osteoblasts, nibbling away at this new and unwanted bone — a bit like bone-eating 'Pacman'! Often I would reinforce this by using a finger or two to touch the area I was working on in my mind. I feel sure that this use of Imagery was another helpful step in my recovery.

Years later, I helped a young girl battle an almost overwhelming brain cancer. When she first came, her mother had been told that Ellie was not responding to treatment, that nothing more could be done for her and that she only had weeks to live. She did a series of drawings with me and when she drew her bedroom, it seemed to me to contain an image that powerfully represented her cancer. Amongst her bedroom furniture she drew her dressing table with a large mirror above it. Here Ellie made the only discordant image in her drawing — she scribbled heavily, angrily, wildly all over the mirror. Outside she had drawn a happy garden and a clothes line. So we put these images together.

Ellie was instructed to close her eyes, imagine the house and the clothesline. In her mind she went to the back of the house, collected a bucket, filled it with water and then took a cleaning rag off the clothes line. She then walked into the house, up into her bedroom (which she had drawn on the first floor) and proceeded to wash off the mirror. The cloth became quite dirty, and she rinsed it in the bucket until the mirror was clean. Then she returned outside, flushed the dirty water down the gully trap, rinsed the cloth and hung it on the line.

Now Ellie had begun this in early December, being blind in one eye already, and her mother having been told that there was little hope of her living to Christmas. Early in the New Year not only was Ellie feeling much better but her sight was back to normal! Then late in January a new development. Ellie's mother rang me, very disturbed, saying that having been in the routine of diligently practising her Imagery morning and evening every day, suddenly Ellie had stopped, saying that she did not want to do it any more. Now it seemed to her unnecessary and a waste of time. Ellie's mother was quite anxious, but I told her that often as people's physical condition changed, their Imagery also could change. As recommended she returned to her doctors and thorough tests found that all the cancer had disappeared! Ellie had made a remarkable recovery!

On the other hand, I well remember a middle aged woman, June, who was coming to our groups at about that same time. Faced with advanced secondary breast cancer, June had been holding her situation stable for eighteen months. In many ways this was a remarkable achievement; yet she grew impatient, a little frustrated. Her husband Ken then told me that he accompanied June to a remarkable meeting with her cancer specialist. June was intent on finding out her prognosis. She wanted to know how long the doctor thought she would live. Ken said that the doctor was very reluctant to commit himself. He pointed out how well June was doing, and how he had not expected her to live as long as she had, but that obviously something she was doing was working very well and she should keep it up. However, June was not going to be put off and kept on demanding a prognosis. Ken said that it seemed to him that in the end, almost in frustration, the doctor said as a throw away line, 'Well, I guess three months would be a good bet.' June died three months later to the day! Ken remains convinced that June fixed that day in her mind as the day of her death and fulfilled the image planted there. It was, he said, as if she had suffered from the 'pointing of the bone', the ritualistic Aboriginal punishment that reliably leads to death with no physical cause or reason involved.

So the experience is that Imagery is a double-edged sword. While it is very potent in its action, Imagery can have constructive or destructive effects. And while we are subjected to the images that are presented to us every moment of our waking, and even sleeping life, when we come to use these images by conscious choice, we need to be confident that we are using them in the correct way. There is a real caution in its use and an imperative for you to feel confident that when you use Imagery in a premeditated way that the images you use are accurate, complete and that the practice is conducted in a positive state of mind.

For this is definitely a field of inner work where there is a right and a wrong way. Over many years now I have worked with many people who have used Imagery in their lives. We have learnt through experience, through mistakes, through successes. What I have found is that there are several major areas where Imagery can have dramatic benefits. Also, what I have found is that, in my view, many of the instructions available for learning Imagery appear incomplete. Often they shout the positive possibilities, which are wonderful, but they neglect to mention the very real pitfalls, or give instruction on how to deal with the problems that easily can arise.

It is easy to find basic information, yet many people who begin to practise Imagery tell me that they have had unexpected experiences which the book or tapes do not cover and which at the very least can be quite disconcerting, or at worst, are downright scary. On top of all this is the fact that if you were to listen to some Imagery exercises and were able to follow through and achieve what some tapes direct, you would end up in perfect health, with the perfect partner and job, incredibly wealthy and happy and probably fully enlightened as well — overnight of course!

So what is real? What is possible? What is fantasy?

Many people also tell me that when they begin to use Imagery, they do so with high hopes. However, often they become confused or even disenchanted, as doubts, unexpected and sometimes disturbing images mingle with what they had expected to be a simple and powerfully positive experience.

One of the main intentions of this book then is to range over the very wide experiences that are possible; to indicate what is normal and reasonable; and to attend to what is unusual and problematical. The emphasis will be on problem solving and the effective use of this exciting technique. Exciting because the positive benefits are very real. While I start by sounding genuinely cautious, I have direct experience of Imagery playing a significant role in improving performance in a wide range of human activities; effectively and positively changing deep-seated, destructive behaviours into constructive ones; powerfully fulfilling creative goals; enhancing wellbeing; being a catalyst in profound healing and deepening spirituality in a transformative and sustainable way.

This then is intended to be a practical book. As said already, it is based upon my own range of life experiences which include a history of competing seriously in athletics, a professional life as a veterinarian, surviving supposedly terminal cancer and then assisting over 10,000 people directly with an innovative cancer self-help program. As well I have worked directly with healthy top flight athletes and business people.

In addition to running many workshops on Imagery, I have noticed Imagery's affects in my own daily life, with its impact on my relationship with my wife Grace and our four children.

Unashamedly then, this book is based primarily on direct experience. While I have read widely on the subject, studied it, attended other people's workshops, and learnt directly from some remarkable teachers, my main teachers have been my own life experience and the many people who have worked cooperatively on Imagery with me. The theories expounded to explain the nature of Imagery, how it affects us and why it works, are, to me, common sense explanations of a basic human function. We all use Imagery all the time. Most of us, it seems, do so with very little training or even, in truth, with little understanding.

What I hope to do in this book is to crystallize what I have learnt and offer it in the spirit of helpful sharing.

What that all means is the purpose of the book — read on!

Now a final proviso. Everything you read in this book may be incorrect!

Incorrect?! Why would I say that, you should well ask? Well, in this field particularly, you need to know that while Imagery (and Affirmations) are powerful, it is still quite possible to simply learn the techniques and use them. However, I believe that as these techniques are using the creative power of your own mind, you need to own them. You do need to take time to consider, reflect and understand. For two reasons. Firstly it is best if you take responsibility for your own actions — and achievements! Secondly, because the more you understand and believe in what you are doing, the more effective it will be.

So I will attempt to give you the best of what I know on all this. I invite you to discriminate. Experiment. Use what feels good and what resonates with your own integrity. Use what works and happily let go of anything else.

I do welcome correspondence on all this and if any questions or difficulties arise, either myself or my wonderful colleagues at The Gawler Foundation would be happy to help. Of course, it is good to hear of what works, and of your successes. For that is the essence of the book — the lessons learnt by both ordinary and remarkable people who have used the Creative Power of Imagery to good effect.

CHAPTER 2

YOUR INNER WORLD

Exercises, definitions, theory and fun!

Let us begin with some simple, yet instructive exercises. Just wherever you are right now, take a few moments to imagine a big dog. It may well help to close your eyes, just allow an image to form in your mind of a big dog and then take a few moments to record what presents itself.

Do the exercise now.

When you open your eyes again the first thing is to notice what feeling went with the image. Was it a warm and happy feeling, or was it an uneasy, even fearful one? In most groups, it seems that the feeling response to the simple image of a large dog is about fifty-fifty. Half seem to like it and feel good about big dogs, the others feel unpleasant, often anxious with even just imagining a big dog.

So we learn straight away that many images are very personal and that often they will have different meanings, different effects, different memories for different individuals.

However, there are some images which can be described better as being Archetypal. Archetypal means a primordial, or fundamental image that is inherited by all. In other words, an image such as water, will have the same meaning to a middle European, to an Australian Aboriginal or a Chinese person. They will all relate to it in a similar way — as a symbol of cleansing, purity, the water of life, a vehicle of spirit.

What we need to realize from this is that when you are using Imagery, unless you are using Archetypal symbols, you are best advised to develop and use images and symbols that are personally relevant and accurate. This again is why it is well worthwhile to have some knowledge and preparation before you begin Imagery practice. This is what I hope to be able to help you with throughout the book.

Back to the image of the big dog — we can learn more from it. What sort of dog was it? What were its features? What was it doing? In what context did you imagine it? Was it like a dog in space — was it just the dog you imagined with no background — or was it in a particular setting, like in a house, a garden, or a street? What were the details of your particular image?

It can be quite fun to ask some members of your family or friends to do this same exercise and to find out what they came up with. The diversity, the different range of images is bound to both amaze and fascinate you.

Now importantly, here is another key. There is no right or wrong in this. One person's image cannot claim to be better or worse than another's. It can rightfully claim to be different, however. So, again, very quickly we can notice the differences in both the details and the feelings that go with particular images, for particular people.

Take another moment now for this next, short exercise. This one is best done with your eyes closed and only takes about a minute. Just wherever you happen to be, after you read this short introduction, simply close your eyes and notice what you are thinking about, notice what thoughts are coming into your mind at this particular time.

Do the exercise now.

You may have read another of my books, *Meditation — Pure & Simple*, where we use this exercise as a starting point to lead into the stillness of deep meditation. For some people, the remarkable thing that happens when they do this simple exercise is that their thoughts clear and they experience a few moments of inner stillness and peace — very directly, very effectively. However, that is not what the aim is here! We do actually want to come up with some thoughts so that we can find out how we notice them! If you found you were one of those people whose thoughts did clear into stillness doing this short exercise, at least you now have a great way to still your mind — simply observe your thoughts as an impartial observer and there you are! What could be simpler? It is worth pointing out that for some, meditation can be just that simple; for others this provides a starting point that *Meditation — Pure & Simple* will help to develop.

Can I suggest, however, that when you did this short exercise just now, whether thoughts were noticeable for you or not, you take a moment now for another short exercise. This time think of what you might do tomorrow. Again, it is probably best to close your eyes and then simply think about what you will do tomorrow. However, as these thoughts come to mind, aim to notice how it is that you are registering the thoughts; how is it that you are aware that you are thinking?

Do the exercise now.

What did you notice? Thinking of what you might do tomorrow, were you aware of the thoughts because you were noticing pictures in your mind, almost like watching video clips running through your head? Or was it more as if you were talking yourself through it, as if there was a conversation going on in your head? Or was it more like you were feeling as if you actually were doing the things? Perhaps you had one or two or even all three running at once?

It is probably worth taking a few more moments, just to check. So again, when you are ready, close your eyes and think about what you might do tomorrow. As these thoughts come to mind, notice how it is that you register them. Do you see them as pictures, hear them as words, or feel them like physical sensations?

Do the exercise now.

What you learn from these simple exercises, is which element of Imagery is naturally predominant for you. Which one was it? Which did you notice most — pictures, words or feelings? Again, it is interesting to compare with others and notice the individual differences.

Another more important thing to notice is the fact that our thoughts do come into our awareness as images. And not only thoughts. Another exercise: Take a few more moments to recall the house that you lived in ten years ago. Probably best to close your eyes again and then recall your house of ten years ago.

Do the exercise now.

So how did you recall it? Did you see pictures of it? Did you see it from the outside? If so did you include the garden or the street? Or was it just the house you saw as if it was surrounded by black space? Did you see the inside? If so, which room or rooms did you see? Did you travel through it? Did you see yourself in the picture or was it as if you were looking at your house in the way you look at things normally — as if through your own eyes? Perhaps though, you recalled your house by talking about it. If so, what were the words? Were you talking to yourself: 'Where was I now; oh yes, ten years ago, I must have been nineteen, etc. etc. Or perhaps you recall it in a more kinesthetic, feeling way and felt yourself in the house or felt the atmosphere of the house itself? And what emotions came with the Image? Did you feel happy, sad, neutral? Notice what an effect a simple image can have on the way you feel.

What this last exercise does do is to demonstrate the key role Imagery plays in the function of our memories. Memories are retrieved as images.

In fact, there is more, for it demonstrates that that part of the mind where memory dwells, the unconscious realm of the mind, has its own language — the language of images. This is another key observation because the unconscious realm of the mind plays such an important role in our everyday life. As well as strong memory, the unconscious holds our conditioning, our habits, and our beliefs. We will explore the crucial relevance of all this to our behaviour, happiness and health throughout the book.

For now it is enough to recognize this significant principle and to observe that often we do not have much direct or conscious communication with our unconscious mind. While it can exert powerful effects for good or bad, be constructive or destructive in our lives and also hold a huge reservoir of wisdom, for many people the gap between their conscious and unconscious minds is like that between two computers that speak different languages — like the IBMs and Apple Macs of old!

What this all means is that if we choose to draw on the huge potential of our unconscious mind, to use it effectively and wisely, we need a way of communicating with it. In computer terms we need an interface! So this is a key principle of mind power — in Imagery we have a common language that has the potential to connect the conscious mind to the unconscious. Because the unconscious mind always functions using Imagery and the conscious mind quite easily can learn to use or interpret images, we have the common language. This is a fact we will put to good use in several of the powerful applications of Imagery throughout the book.

However, before we move on to the practical uses of Imagery, it is well to define some terms. This too is important because you may well have read or heard the words Imagery,

Visualisation and Affirmations and wondered what each really meant.

The Oxford Dictionary defines Imagery as 'mental images collectively.' An image is defined as an 'artificial imitation of the external form of an object, a mental representation, a simile or metaphor or the character of a thing or person as perceived by the public'!

To imagine is defined as meaning to 'form mental images or concept of, to picture to oneself (something non-existent or not present to the senses), to think or conceive.'

Given all that, how I would like to define and use the word *Imagery* in this book, is to describe it as the 'conscious development and repetition of mental images for a creative purpose.'

Now again, be reminded that these creative effects can be constructive or destructive, depending on the application of the techniques. Furthermore, as we have learnt already, images are composed predominantly of pictures, words and feelings. While the senses of taste and smell can add to Imagery, they are not so relevant as the three major senses of sight (pictures), sound (words), touch (feelings or sensations).

Visualisation in the way I use the term, only involves the use of inner pictures, while Affirmation is the use of the power of words for their own often remarkable effects.

So, to be clear, Imagery may for some people be practised primarily using only pictures or only words or only feelings. Most people are predominant in one of these three. However, the more of the five senses that can be developed and combined into any Imagery exercise, the more potent that exercise becomes. So we will return to how to expand your Imagery in the most complete and effective way with the different exercises still to come. But clearly, Visualisation uses only pictures, Affirmations only words, Imagery — all the senses possible!

The next exercise, however, will demonstrate another of the natural ways in which we use Imagery every day. Imagine that for your next holiday, you will have the time and money to go on the best trip you could ever hope for! Take a few moments now to indulge this fantasy. Close your eyes, consider your choices, and plan your trip. Where will you go? How will you get there? What will you do once you are there?

Do the exercise now.

So what did you decide? Where did you choose to go? How did you get there? What did you do, and importantly too, how did all this feel? Did you feel a sense of delight with this simple fantasy? Did you feel a sense of frustration or disappointment, doubting the possibility or practicality of such a holiday trip? Are you about to run out and make the bookings?! Again, notice the impact that is made upon you by the suggestion to ponder a particular thought. Notice too that it is Imagery that you use for the thinking, for the planning.

As you consider the choices, in this case the range of holiday possibilities, it is Imagery that is used to review the possibilities. Once you make your choice and plan how to get there, again it is Imagery that is the key to the process of how you do it.

So, planning too is done using Imagery. What type of images predominated for you in this particular exercise? Pictures, words or feelings? Did any taste or smell come into it? Want to check? Take a few more moments to fantasize over the trip you might take for your next holiday. Notice how you consider the choices, fix on one particular trip and plan how you could do it. It will all be done with images. Just check out now how you do it and what type of Imagery you are using.

Do the exercise now.

This exercise begins to reveal the very nature of the mind itself. Basically, if you reflect upon it, it is very evident that our mind's key role is to help us to survive. The fact that we humans are so dominant on this planet certainly is not due to us being physically the strongest or fastest or toughest. No, our dominant feature is our mind, with its capacity to register experiences, record them, learn from them and then apply what we have learnt in new situations — all with the intention of doing whatever will give us the best chance of surviving, and the best chance of being most happy.

Perhaps the easiest way to understand how the mind works in this way, is to consider the holiday trip again. Do this as a simple fantasy exercise, and just so that you can notice your mind at work. Consider again where you might really go for a coming holiday. There are probably many destinations you could choose from. Reflect a little and make a choice. As you do this, you reveal one of the fundamental principles of how the mind works. Eventually you choose one destination. You make a goal. Then planning becomes possible, it flows on naturally and the result you hope for (of actually getting there) also becomes a possibility. This then demonstrates to us that the mind is goal-orientated, e.g. the mind likes to have a clear goal, then it can begin to make the decisions, the choices that will most likely lead to that goal being fulfilled.

We can best describe it by saying that the mind is a goal orientated, decision-making tool. A tool that we ideally use in the most effective way possible!

So with the trip, once a goal is decided upon, once you have selected your destination, then it is time for the details: Will you drive, go by train, fly? What will it cost? Have you enough money already or how will you get it? When do you need to book? What will you take? On and on the planning goes as you do whatever it takes to fill in all the necessary steps to get from where you are now to where you want to be — to fulfilling this goal.

These simple observations on how the mind works in fact do reveal two of the vital principles of what many people call *positive thinking*. However, altogether, there are three.

The three principles of positive thinking

1. Develop a clear goal.

2. Do whatever it takes to achieve that goal.

3. Choose to enjoy doing it!

The third principle — enjoying doing it — is so important as it relates to our feelings. If it does not feel good, it is not likely that we will persist for long, whereas if we are enjoying it, and we are doing whatever it takes, we are almost assured of success. But realize that the operative word is 'Choose' — choose to enjoy doing it. Recognize the power of choice. For while in most situations if you have a clear goal, and are committed to it and are doing whatever it takes, you are almost certain to enjoy it; there may be other situations where it is tough going, there are hurdles to overcome, or where a lot of perseverance is required. Remember then that you have your own power of choice. You can choose to be happy, to be sad, to be depressed or joyful. That choice is yours alone. You may feel initially that circumstances dictate how you 'should' feel. However, be assured that you do have this great freedom, perhaps the only true freedom, the freedom to decide how you will react to your circumstances — the freedom to decide how you will feel.

Now this is not an invitation to suppress feelings. But it is an invitation not to get stuck with them. So, faced with any type of difficult situation you may well feel sad or depressed. That could be both natural and reasonable. It is probably important, perhaps even almost essential, to acknowledge and share those feelings with others, before you decide to move on and to set a new goal.

It may well be very helpful to more fully acknowledge the full extent of the difficulties and to share the feelings that go with them before you are really free to decide more actively how you will respond to the situation. Then you will be freer to determine to do whatever it takes to fulfill your new goal and to choose to enjoy doing it!

I well remember my old friend George who provides a classic and very real example of all this. George was diagnosed with prostate cancer many years ago. George had left his home country and travelled half-way around the world to start a new life at the age of nineteen. He worked hard, married, raised a family and eventually developed a successful business. When George's cancer was diagnosed he was devastated. It was very advanced, widely spread through his bones and his doctors only gave him months to live. George stopped work, locked himself in his house, and with the blinds closed, spent most of the day crying. He did not talk to his wife or children when they came home in the evening. He put all his energy into suppressing his feelings, fears and tears, while he attempted to put on a brave, exterior front. Inside, however, he felt like a man just waiting to die.

Time passed painfully slowly. Then one day he went out for the paper and his eyes fell on my first book *You Can Conquer Cancer*. His eyes lit up with the title, he bought it, read it and thought perhaps it was worth a try. George came to our groups and felt the hope rise within him. He began to talk about it all with his wife, then his children. They shared something of their grief and fear. They cried together. But then, with a new sense of possibility, they resolved to do something about it. George now had a goal. He believed that it was possible to get well again — he could imagine himself not only surviving, but enjoying life again. George did many things, worked hard with great commitment and excellent support. He went on to have a remarkable recovery.

A final two exercises to clarify another key point regarding how the mind works. Both these experiments take only a minute. So for the first, just close your eyes again and this time spend a minute not thinking of a white horse. That's right, a minute *not* thinking of a white horse!

Do the exercise now.

How did you go? For most people, that white horse just keeps on charging into their thoughts. It seems that trying not to think of it, just draws attention to it and makes it more of a focus.

So now the second of these experiments. This time spend a minute thinking of a red rose. You can pay close attention to the details — do you imagine a rose in space, or is it in a vase, or on a bush, or is it with someone? Is your rose a bud or is it in full bloom? Perhaps you can even imagine its perfume or feel the stem or petals. Just take a minute now to concentrate on a red rose.

Do the exercise now.

Probably this is an easy task to manage. Focusing on a red rose for a minute is usually easy enough. This second exercise also holds the key to the white horse. The most effective way to *not* think of something, is to think of something else.

Most importantly, we need to be aware that *not* thinking of something actually focuses the goal-orientated mind on that very thing — just as effectively as if you had chosen to think of it directly! So you can observe this principle at work when parents tell their children 'Don't walk in the puddles!' This draws the kids' attention to the puddles and in they go! And then the parents have the cheek to get upset after they have quite effectively, if somewhat unconsciously, directed them straight in! So, how do you tell a child to keep out of the puddles? Think of it for a moment. The mind is a goal-orientated decision-making tool. You want the mind to focus away from the puddles. Where do you want the child to go? On the dry ground. So you say 'Keep on the dry ground.'

Have you ever seen a child carrying a full bowl of soup? What is the natural reaction? To shout 'Don't spill the soup!' But what is it that the mind registers? 'Spill' and 'soup.' So when the soup is spilled, there is just as likely to be another insult added to the injury. 'You clumsy kid, why didn't you do what I told you?' The poor child not only feels guilty for making a mess but gets a negative affirmation as well. If the child was really smart, he should reply to the parent, 'But I did, I did just what you told my mind to do!'

So how do you tell someone not to spill the soup? Think again — what do you want them to do?

Try 'Keep the bowl level!' It works just about every time.

These examples are fun yet quite important. Most children are barraged with negative affirmations as they grow up and are focused inappropriately in this way.

Likewise in adult conversations or at work, most of us have been taught to use the 'Don't do this or don't do that' style. So, it can be very useful to listen to yourself and then make the effort to retrain yourself to use positive affirmations or directions. This can be done, but for most it takes a lot of practice; so be gentle as you start to retrain yourself!

This same principle can be extremely important in healing. Many people facing life-threatening illness, begin by being scared of dying. This is not surprising and often this fear leads to a high motivation to get well. However, if the focus is 'I don't want to die,' from the mind's point of view, what is the target, what is the goal? Obviously the dying! So, what is an important step in getting well? Shifting the focus onto living! What does the person want to live for? What is the reason for living? What is the passion?

This is obvious in George's graphic case. While he was feeling hopeless and full of the fear of dying, he was hoping not to die but literally all he was doing was waiting around for it to happen. Once he became inspired and felt that there was some hope for recovery, he was able to rekindle his natural love of life and set about living again. Healing began to flow almost immediately.

Therefore, in comparison with trying not to die, there is far more healing in focusing on living and living well! As we study all this, we soon come to realize that we are healed by what we turn towards, far more than what we turn away from. When we affirm life, healing is a much greater possibility. And while healing so graphically demonstrates this principle, we can notice how this is another feature of the mind and the use of Imagery that is of great importance in every other aspect of life.

Here then is a summary of what we have learnt in this introduction:

- The mind's creative power is vast, while its effects can be destructive or constructive depending upon how it is used.

- All the workings of the mind involve the use of images.

- Imagery is the conscious development and repetition of mental images for a creative purpose.

- Through Imagery we can dramatically increase the creative power of our mind.

- Images can be personal or archetypal. Personal images will have different effects on different individuals. Archetypal images have a more universal impact.

- Inner images primarily are made up of words, pictures and feelings. The other senses may be relevant, but commonly are less involved.

- Feelings are an integral part, in fact a key part of the effective use of Imagery.

- Thoughts come to our awareness via images.

- Memories are recalled using images.

- Planning is carried out using images.

- Communication between the conscious and unconscious aspects of the mind is possible using the common language of Imagery.

- The mind is a goal-orientated, decision-making tool.

- There are three principles of Positive Thinking:
  1. Develop a clear goal.
  2. Do whatever it takes to achieve that goal.
  3. Choose to enjoy doing it!

- The mind, as a goal-orientated tool, targets onto whatever is in strongest focus. Importantly, this focus can be expressed as a positive or a negative — the red rose or the white horse.

- What we turn our focus towards has far more importance than what we are attempting to turn away from. Focus on the positive, the creative side of life!

Now that we have some understanding of the way our mind works, and the basic principles behind Imagery, let us move on to how we can prepare to use Creative Imagery techniques consciously and effectively!

CHAPTER 3

SETTING CLEAR GOALS

The wisdom behind Imagery

This to me is the trickiest part of the whole process. While the actual need for having a clear goal may seem obvious — it is how to clarify those goals and how to decide what goals are really in your best interests that pose the deepest and most challenging questions. Get this answer right and everything else is easy! So, given that you have decided to go on a holiday it may be easy enough to decide which destination you will go to. But what if you were to pause long enough to fully consider what else you could do with the time and money if you did not go on a holiday at all. Then the possibilities open up endlessly. You could save the money, stay home and sleep. You could give some of the money away to a worthwhile cause and go on a retreat. You could borrow more money, stay home and spend the time extending the house. You could … You could …

So how do you decide? Are you a creature of habit who goes on holidays because it is Christmas and that is what you always do? Do you rationalize the balance of work, play, rest and holidays and make a calculated choice? Do you go because the children demand it? Is someone else making your choices for you? Are you making them yourself? And if you are, on what basis are your choices being made?

These are the sort of irritating and slightly provocative questions that most of us prefer to defer. We probably put off the thinking and go simply because it feels like a good idea at the time! No real harm done with a holiday. But what if we use the same approach for 'Which job will I take?', 'Where would

I prefer to live?', 'What lifestyle will I adopt?' Clearly, the big question is how to decide what goals to pursue? Perhaps it is worth taking a few moments to review your whole decision making process.

The first thing is to notice who sets your goals. Is it you, or is it other people? Often this question is helped by actually contemplating the question 'Who is living my life?' Who tells me what to do directly? Or subtly? Who am I attempting to please? Or hurt? Who influences the decisions I make? Who affects how I live my life?

To contemplate 'Who is living my life?', sit quietly as you might if you were in the practice of meditating, close your eyes, relax a little and begin to ask yourself the question 'Who is living my life?' Perhaps the first thing you think of is 'Wow, actually other people are doing it for me quite a lot.' If so, think of who those people might be. Consider them one at a time. Imagine them doing the things they do for or to you, reflecting on how it is that each particular person is dictating terms in your life. Making decisions for you, living your life. Keep asking yourself 'Who is living my life?' and looking deeply into the answers, the people who come in response to the question.

Perhaps it is almost as if these people who are living your life make up a committee that collectively is in charge of your life. The committee tells you when you are OK, when what you are doing or thinking is OK, when you got it wrong, when you need to suffer! What a lot of power these people can have. A great Imagery exercise can be to imagine all the people on your particular committee, gather them together, and then put them on a bus. Take them for a long drive. Put them off the bus! Whoopee! Put a sign up on the front of the bus. No passengers! Leave the committee behind. Start driving your own bus!

We often do this type of exercise another way in our groups. You may find this both helpful, fun and therapeutic after having done the contemplation exercise. Take a sheet of A4 paper and turn it on its side. Make a small egg shape in the middle and write 'ME' in it. Now draw pencil lines radiating like spokes to other eggs circling your own. In these outer eggs write the names of the people who live your life for you. Parents, children, partner, boss, employees, bank manager, lady over the back fence, etc. You may need a few layers of 'eggs' to fit them all in! When you have completed the task, get a rubber and determine to make a change. Erase the connecting ties and as you do so, let each person go, inwardly as well as in this more ritual way. It could be the start of a whole new phase of your life.

This simple technique has some similarity in intention and effect to a process developed by Phyllis Krystal and detailed in her book *Cutting the Ties that Bind*. Many people are finding this a powerfully effective way of letting go of unhealthy bonds and in so doing, becoming free to develop more (truly) intimate and adult relationships.

To continue, if you are to make your own decisions, set your own goals, how can you be confident that you are on the right track? Do you just 'go with the flow' and allow circumstances around you to decide? Do you attempt to reason it all out and be very logical? Do you hope for revealing insight and the assurance of wisdom?

In practical reality, you probably use a bit of everything, but when it comes to the crunch, the guts rule! Many decisions are dependent upon other people, many are made on the run in response to immediate pressures, influences and opportunities. Reason is useful and wisdom sometimes prevails. However, over and above all this is the fact that what feels good at the time is likely to be a major deciding factor. There is a real secret in this — what is it that makes for that good feeling?

When we practise Imagery, we are using a premeditated process for a particular purpose. In this situation, more deliberation is often warranted and certainly highly recommended. The intellect remains a great asset and it would seem an ideal if we could complement it with a deeper wisdom to set our major goals. So while some people have a natural wisdom that seems to flow effortlessly, most of us experience our innate wisdom sporadically. So, how to develop our inner wisdom and draw on its potential when we need to review or set goals? And can we do this in a way that we can trust the outcome? In a way that we can feel happy with the goal and confidently commit to following it through? There are three major possibilities.

Techniques for Clarifying your Goals

These are three reliable techniques for accessing your inner wisdom that can be learnt relatively easily and in my experience work well for people — the stillness of meditation, specific Insight Meditation and Inner Wisdom Imagery.

1.   Meditation and goal setting

One of the most common benefits people notice and describe to me when they begin meditation, is that decisions now seem easier to make, they feel more confident of them and that these decisions actually do work better for them in the full context of their lives.

Barry was a reasonably successful small business man who came to learn meditation with a desperate sense of needing to control stress. He was sleeping poorly, he was irritable and felt a constant nagging unease which he came to know as a vague, widespread but ill-defined fear. Barry began to meditate and each time I saw him his smile became easier, more constant and wider. He reported with amazement how the fear just seemed to be melting. He could not say what happened to it, he had not addressed it directly, he was not sure where it went, but he was sure that it was going! In its place was a new-found confidence that warmed his smile. He was deeply impressed with the change in his decision-making — gone were the anxieties and doubts, now it seemed so easy.

And the results were delightful. Within a short space of time his business improved so dramatically that he won a major small business award.

Why then would meditation help goal setting? Well, if you are affected by stress, it is almost certain that you will be under-reacting or over-reacting. Stress clouds judgement, tension creates strain and depletes energy. Meditation on the other hand, helps you to regain a more natural state of balance and to be free to react appropriately. Meditation leads to a clear state of mind and naturally allows wisdom to flow. So, without addressing the issue specifically, the regular practice of meditation can lead to good decision making.

If you prefer to be more actively involved in the conscious act of decision making, and perhaps to add to the benefits of passive meditation anyway, there are two specific techniques I can recommend.

2.   Insight Meditation

Insight Meditation is an age-old technique for problem solving, goal setting, and the gaining of insight. I wrote a good deal about it, and how to do it, in a major section of *Peace of Mind*. Here let us summarize how to use it in the context of goal setting.

So that we can investigate how this technique works, let us use the example of reviewing your eating habits and deciding on what sort of diet to follow. Here are the steps:

1.   Decide what the issue is (e.g. in this case to set dietary goals) and determine to reach a conclusion.

2.   Do the research. Use your intellect. Read the books, speak to the experts, discuss it with friends, listen to tapes. Ideally make notes. This person said that; this book the other, etc. With food it is usually easiest to write out lists of the different recommendations.

3.   Set a time for the decision to be made. If you were to buy a new washing machine, probably you could wait until

you have gathered all the relevant information. Presuming you have determined your price range, you can find out the makes and models that are available and collect all their details within a reasonable period of time. However, with food you could collect information almost indefinitely. So you probably need to say to yourself something like 'I will collect all the information I can in the next two weeks (this two weeks is just an arbitrary figure I have used — there is no need to take me literally on this one!) and then I will make the best decision I can.'

4.   On the day when the decision is to be made, give yourself some time — half an hour to an hour is ideal — and some space — either where you meditate regularly or in any quiet area. Make sure that you can be free from the telephone and other possible distractions. Take with you any notes that you have made and any other material you have gathered. Also take a pen and some paper in case you want to write on it.

5.   When you sit down, begin by reviewing your research material and in this way refreshing all the knowledge you have of your subject. If you do not have any written material, go straight on to the next step.

6.   Consciously relax your body and calm your mind. This will be a familiar process if you have some experience of meditation. The aim is to elicit the Relaxation Response so that you are in a better state of mind to progress into Insight Meditation. If this is new to you, you can follow the details on pages 68–76 of this book, or have a more complete introduction by reading *Peace of Mind* and *Meditation — Pure and Simple*.

7.   Once relaxed in this manner, focus your attention on consciously reviewing the facts as you remember them.

So, in our example, you might recall the style of food you have been eating, the broad issues relating to why you are considering changing your diet, what different people have recommended to you, what you have read in different books and so on.

If at any stage you become distracted or your mind wanders off onto other thoughts, as soon as you recognize this, be gentle on yourself and simply come back to concentrating on issues relating to food and diet.

This first part of the process then is clearly a rational, left brain exercise.

What happens next, as you continue to concentrate on the topic, is that at some point you will automatically shift into more abstract, intuitive, right brain contemplation. It will be as if all the facts you have been reflecting upon and analysing, all the pieces of the jigsaw puzzle as it were, come together and now you can clearly see the bigger picture. This gives a new sense of comprehension and understanding and usually leaves you with a clear sense of what to do. This can all come with a moment of clear insight, almost like an 'Ah Ha! I've got it' moment of revelation.

The more you practise this technique, the more reliable it becomes. It is a wonderful and dependable way to solve problems, develop creativity and instigate lateral thinking.

8.   Once the sense of clarity dawns, usually it is best to write the ensuing insight down. Perhaps you can remember having had the experience of a moment of insight like this before. Perhaps you were in the shower or was it when you were half asleep, and suddenly like a bolt out of the blue, it seemed as if you have the perfect solution to a problem you had been wrestling with. Yet by the time you got dressed and had breakfast, it had flown from your memory! Insight Meditation sometimes can be like that too, so it is best to write it down. I always do this exercise with pen and paper close by and as soon

as the answer begins to form — write it down. As
another aside, this is an excellent way to prepare for and
complete creative writing.

This Insight Meditation technique can be used to solve any
problem. It leads to a clarity that is backed by a deep sense of
your own inner wisdom. As a result, the directions that come
with it, the goals that emerge from this exercise, feel very
'right' for you. They are easy to feel confident about, easy to
commit to. And very commonly, they do work well!

Now for an Imagery exercise that is even more creative!

3.   Inner Wisdom (or Inner Guide) Imagery

This is an exercise we have found to be profoundly useful
and effective in our residential programs. In that setting,
amidst the atmosphere of time out from the busyness and
distractions of daily life, and with the support of trained staff,
many people have gained major insights through this process. The exercise is included here as people have been able to
benefit from it directly, and it is quite a detailed technique.

First a little background. Scientifically, it is widely recognized
that everything we ever learnt or experienced is stored in our
memory. A few rare individuals have what we call
photographic memories with virtually total recall. Most of us
struggle a bit with better or worse memories. The good news,
however, is that it is all in there — the only question is how to
gain access to it.

You may have had some experience of being confronted with a
major problem that almost demanded a solution, yet you were
not quite sure what to do. Or perhaps there was the sense of
having the answer 'on the tip of your tongue' — a sense of the
solution being there, inside somewhere, but just out of reach!
You may have had the experience of working hard for the
solution, researching, questioning, reading, reflecting. All to no
avail until almost in frustration, you let it all go. Perhaps you
were having a shower, walking in a park, or in that gentle

reverie half way between sleep and awake. Then POW! It almost seems to hit you and there it is — the answer, so simple, so obvious, so clear! Most of us have had this experience at some time in our lives, yet for most of us, this process occurs infrequently and somewhat unpredictably.

The following Inner Wisdom Imagery exercise aims to provide a structured way into that same level of wisdom, insight and clarity. And it also has a more profound possibility. A common psychological theory, made particularly popular by Carl Jung, is that there is a *collective unconscious*. Just as we have our own Inner Wisdom accumulated by our range of personal experience, there is a vast body or reservoir of collective human experience. The theory is that this is like a mainframe computer with all the experience of the ages stored in it. Our own mind is like a PC that has the potential to tap into the larger unit! Now you may quite reasonably question the truth of all this but the delightful thing about meditation in general, and this Inner Wisdom Imagery exercise in particular, is that it provides you with a means to investigate and find out for yourself.

The feature of this exercise is that when it works, as it does often, the responses that you get, the Insights that it provides, will have a certainty that can only be gained through direct experience. If you do this exercise and need to question whether the answers you receive are valid and real or not, then do question them deeply. For it is possible to do this exercise in the sense of wish fulfilment, to keep it on the emotional/rational level and get from it what you had hoped for or expected in a fairly superficial way.

The real opportunity with this exercise is to go beyond the thinking mind, to connect more directly with your own wisdom mind and perhaps even to go beyond all this, and connect with the vast collective unconscious. Answers that come from that place come with a certainty beyond the need for questioning. They come with an assured sense of knowing. Often when this happens, major insights occur that can help you to understand more of your life, why you are like you are and what you can do to solve major issues affecting your life.

What we are aiming to do then, is to connect the conscious mind with the unconscious in a way that the two can communicate. As we know already there is a common language which does link the conscious and unconscious minds — Imagery. Using this knowledge, the aim of the Inner Wisdom Imagery exercise is to create in our mind an image that represents our Inner Wisdom — an image which our conscious mind can then communicate with, asking questions, seeking and gaining answers.

The Inner Wisdom technique involves two steps. First we create an Inner Sanctuary — an image of a place where we feel particularly peaceful and comfortable. This part of the exercise is often referred to as the Quiet Place. This relaxes us, puts our mind at ease and transports us to an inner world where we are in more direct contact with the unconscious. Then into this Quiet Place we invite an image to join us — an image that will represent our Inner Wisdom. This image can take many forms; it is like an Inner Guide. For some it may be an archetypal old man with long white hair and beard and flowing robes, for others Mother Mary. For some a special person in their life who has died, for others an animal, domesticated or wild. There have been cartoon characters, rocks, even formless clouds with a powerful sense of presence.

The best way to approach this exercise is with the open and attentive mind of experimentation. While it is useful to have your questions clear in your mind at the start, it is best to let go of any expectations as to what the outcome will be. Very often, when you enter into this exercise fully and with an open mind, completely new images, questions and directions can arise spontaneously.

Take time to relax and calm your mind first, then follow the exercise and be interested to notice what happens.

The Inner Wisdom Imagery Exercise

The Quiet Place and Inner Guide

1. Begin by taking time to clarify what your question is. If you have an obvious issue or problem you need a creative solution to, simply formulate it into a question. Perhaps also, you could ponder what question you would ask if you were able to speak directly to your Inner Wisdom — what would that question be?

2. Give yourself the space and time for the exercise — about half an hour is enough, although it is helpful if you have more time available after you finish so that you can simply relax and reflect on the exercise if you want to.

3. The exercise can be done lying down, but probably it is preferable to sit in a chair or on the floor.

4. Take a few moments to consciously relax your body a little in whatever way works best for you.

5. Now, allow an image to form in your mind of a place where you feel particularly peaceful and comfortable. It may be a place that you have been to before; or it may be a fantasy place; just allow an image to form in your mind of a place where you feel particularly peaceful and comfortable — and in a way that we can explore it in more detail.

    Notice firstly where this Quiet Place is. Is it a fantasy place, a composite of several places you know, or one specific place? Be reminded there is no right or wrong in this, just concentrate on this place which is special for you.

    Now what can you see in this place? What is close by? What shapes, what sizes, what colours? What shades of colour? Take your time to enjoy looking at the details, building them up steadily. You will probably notice what time of day it is. If you can see the sky, are there clouds, or is it clear? You probably will also notice if there is any movement or if it is quite still. Really *notice* the details as fully as you can.

Now *listen* for what sounds you can hear in this place. What can you hear nearby or are there any sounds coming from further away? What sounds can you hear in this place?

Give your attention now to noticing what *smells* may be noticeable in this place — what fragrance, what odour, what can you smell in this place?

You will probably be able to *feel* the temperature in this place. Is it warm or cool, or is it neutral? Can you feel any breeze on your skin, or the warmth of the sun on your face? Notice too your position and what you have contact with — is it hard or soft, damp or dry? So notice what physical sensations go with this place.

Be aware that if there is anything that you could change to make this place even more peaceful and comfortable, you could do that.

Now dwell on the *feeling* that comes with being in this place. Allow these feelings to build within you and rest with those feelings for a few moments.

6.   Now imagine that off in the distance a small white cloud or mist is forming and that it begins to move slowly towards you. There is a knowing that within this cloud will be a symbol that represents your Inner Wisdom, your Inner Guide. As the small cloud moves closer to you, the shape of the symbol begins to form and becomes clearly obvious. The symbol may then move out of the cloud and approach you, coming to within a comfortable distance. This is your Inner Guide.

Notice the features of your Inner Guide. Notice what size it is, taking in the details. Perhaps your Guide has a name that you seem to know already.

Perhaps now there is something you would like to say to your Inner Guide. Perhaps there is a question. If so, then ask it. Again, expect a reply.

This may lead to an exchange or perhaps your Inner Guide has something to say to you, perhaps a question for you. You could listen for that.

When you feel ready to take your leave, perhaps there is something you would like to do or say before you go. Perhaps some contact, perhaps some more words, perhaps an arrangement to meet again, perhaps a sense of this Inner Guide, this Inner Wisdom remaining close to you with ready access.

7. Once you have parted, bring your attention back to your Quiet Place, that Inner Sanctuary. Take a few moments to feel yourself in that special place once again. Then probably you will be aware of a part of this place that appeals to you most particularly. If you are not there already, go to that place so that you can rest a while. Lie down, and as you do so, feel your body relaxing completely, so much so that you feel almost as if you could float up a little off the ground. Just resting now for a few moments, floating just a few inches off the ground.

8. When you are ready you can begin to end the exercise. Just be reminded that at any time you choose to in the future you can return to this exercise and that each time you do it will be easier and even more complete.

Now bring your attention back to your body. Feel your toes move a little, move your hands a little, perhaps a deeper breath or two and when you are ready, let your eyes gently open again.

This exercise often leads to major insights and deeply satisfying answers. It can be used regularly, or simply when there is a particular need. It may be helpful to read the extra details on how to start this exercise by developing and using the Quiet Place Imagery in Chapter Seven. While for many people this is an exercise that is straight forward, easy and deeply satisfying, the range of experiences does vary. For some it is a bit of a non-event while for a small few it can lead to images that initially are confusing or disconcerting. These images, although difficult or confronting at first can be very useful in their own right. There are a number of ways to effectively deal with difficult images and this is covered in Chapter Six, but another reminder here. If you feel that you need help you can seek professional help or call me or my staff.

What follows is a dramatic example of this Inner Wisdom Imagery at work. It highlights how often the images have to be worked on to begin with, almost as if the initial images are 'manufactured' or invoked. However, frequently there is then the sense of fully entering into the exercise, in a very real and meaningful way.

Kerry attended an Inward Bound program and had difficulty forming any clear images. She had a very hazy Quiet Place and really struggled to find any image for her Inner Wisdom. As I began to help her directly, a symbolic image of a golden triangle formed. It was filled with a great deal of light. When prompted, Kerry asked this symbol 'Where do I find love?' There was a long pause and a disappointed 'No answer.' Sensing there was a block to all this, I suggested Kerry might like to ask 'Who do I have to forgive?' She felt good with this and asked the question of her Inner Wisdom. The answer came straight back with total clarity, 'Yourself.' I prompted Kerry again, suggesting she might like to ask what she needed to forgive herself for. Again she did this and put the question. Again, an immediate response. 'For being alive!' This came like a thunderbolt to Kerry. It was so powerful and touched such a deep note of recognition in the core of her being that she became very emotional, almost hysterical.

Almost immediately another image came into her awareness. At first it was of her as a child, then an image and feeling that was of the time before she was born. These images were arising quite spontan
eously now. Kerry was simply describing them to me as they formed. She explained that she had a very strong feeling that her mother had not wanted her and that she did not feel welcome to be born.

Later Kerry explained to me that her mother had separated from her father during Kerry's pregnancy. Her mother already had two small children, aged one and two, and had needed to return to her family home for the birth. Her parents were strict Catholics and deeply disapproved of the separation and of having a child with no father present.

What this exercise did for Kerry was to help make sense of why she had become the woman she had. She realized that she had been apologizing all her life for simply being here. Now, through the exercise she realized that it was OK to be alive, that she did deserve to be here.

Kerry also realized that her mother had done the best she could for her at the time. But she was aware that as a child it had been fairly awful and affected her life deeply. Now as an adult she knew she could change. The exercise had clarified some profound issues and given her the goal of actually reclaiming her life. Kerry went on to work hard at forgiving her mother and feels now that she can love her as her mother. She still finds that as a person her mother is difficult for her to be with, and there is ongoing work to do. For herself, Kerry found that this one Imagery exercise quite transformed her, completely reframed a core inner belief and has left her more optimistic, joyful, peaceful and yes, Alive!

The Inner Wisdom exercise therefore is useful for tackling the big questions. Some people do use it on simpler, day to day issues; while most find that the previous two techniques are often more relevant for simple goal setting.

Taken together, the hope is that these goal setting exercises are as useful for you as they are for most and you are ready now to consider some more of the key principles that can be used to make your Imagery fully effective.

CHAPTER 4

THE STARTING POINT

Acknowledge where you are starting from

The mind, as we have discovered already, is a goal-orientated, decision-making tool. When it comes to using it, it is a bit like following a map. You decide upon a destination, a goal. Fixing that goal in mind, you then make a range of choices that appear most likely to lead you to your destination. Along the way, you are quite likely to come to crossroads, diversions, obstacles as well as tranquil, easy stretches. You check your position, you get feedback, assess your progress, make any corrections. All this makes for a useful metaphor.

However, think back to the obvious. When you look up a map, say a street map to find your way across town, before you can begin the journey you need two very important locations — the end point, the destination, the goal — of course. But before you can actually begin the journey, most importantly, you need to find where you are starting from!

This seems to me to be a point often overlooked by people engaged in so-called positive thinking. 'So-called' because to me it is positive to acknowledge the starting point — where you are right now. Presuming you feel the need to be somewhere else, presuming that you want to use positive thinking to move to a new place, to be different, to be better, to be healthier, happy, wealthier, whatever; then presumably there is at least some sense that where you are now is not satisfactory. For this is the joy of positive thinking and Imagery, it can facilitate major personal change and be used with great creative power to set new goals, achieve them and enhance many aspects of life.

Yet many people who embark on all this attempt to gloss over their current problems.

There seems to have been a prevailing view amongst many in the community that to be positive, you are not allowed even a whiff of what we might commonly call a negative emotion. Tears, grief, anger, sadness, rage — all these so-called *negative* emotions seem to have a pretty poor press amongst many 'positive thinkers'.

In my experience, failing to acknowledge where you are starting from, and feeling the emotion of that place, works for only a very small minority. For some, perhaps those people who are so rigid or strong in their thinking, so left brained, analytical and logical, it can work. For most, however, omitting or neglecting this step of acknowledgment leads to a sense of denial; denial that may be helpful for a short while, but often leads to a breakdown and a need to reassess and start again.

The best example that comes to mind to illustrate this point concerns a delightful couple I met interstate. We had arranged to conduct one of our residential cancer self help programs in Perth and this Sydney couple flew across to join it as they were quite desperate. The husband, Martin, had been diagnosed six weeks earlier with bowel cancer and liver secondaries. He had been happily married to his wife Joyce for over forty years and for much of that time they had worked together; by all accounts in a very happy working and personal relationship. A little over a year previously, Martin had been badly betrayed by his business partner and had internalized all his anger, grief and despair. He felt sure in himself that the way he had reacted to this major stress had been a precipitating factor in his illness. At the same time he acknowledged that he had lived a somewhat extravagant lifestyle and was not surprised that the bowel was where his dis-ease showed up.

Joyce had been deeply affected by her husband's diagnosis and she was determined to be the ideal support person for Martin. Joyce loved Martin dearly and was ready to do whatever she could to help. Her idea of what this meant was that she should keep a stiff upper lip, keep her own emotions in, and exude an outer, positive manner.

So for six weeks most of Joyce's energy had been going into attempting to hold her tears back. She felt heartbroken with what had happened, and was deeply shocked by the doctor's dire predictions for the man she loved.

By the time Joyce and Martin's plane landed in Perth and they began to make their way to our program, Joyce said she could feel her knees starting to wobble nervously. As the group began and people made their introductions, it was obvious that both Joyce and Martin were making huge efforts to contain their emotions. At the end of the second day Joyce approached me and said that she felt she really needed to leave the course, book into a motel, wait until the program was over and then return to collect Martin. In response to my obvious enquiry, she explained that she feared that if she stayed any longer she would be completely unable to contain her emotions. She was truly fearful that if she let them out she would open the floodgates and cry a lot. Her real concern, she said, was not for her, but for what impact her emotions would have on Martin. She did not want to appear negative around him; she only wanted to be positive so that she could best help him.

I agreed with her on the need to be positive. Then I put it to her that if I had been married to her for over forty years in what I thought had been a happy marriage, and if I had been diagnosed with a rather nasty form of cancer with a poor medical prognosis; and faced with all this she showed no emotion — I would wonder what I really meant to her, what had gone wrong! I explained to Joyce that her emotional reaction to Martin's diagnosis was very natural and reasonable. Sure, it is true that occasionally partners do react without tears. When I was diagnosed, Grace was a classic example of someone who immediately felt confident of overcoming all possible obstacles and of me recovering. So Grace felt no grief and was not only clear but determined to go forward immediately. I suspect that this degree of certainty is rather rare, and that Joyce's response is more the norm. Importantly, that is not to say one is right or wrong — but clearly the reactions are very different.

It seems to me there are two issues here. The first is the natural response to the situation — the problem as I would call it here. (Some may prefer to call it a challenge or an opportunity, to my simple mind it sure sounds at this stage like a bloody problem! It may be reframed to become a challenge or an opportunity, and that is what I would hope for and expect, but let us deal with what it is like to begin with first). So there is the immediate reaction to the problem, then there is this judgmental part of our mind that comes in and comments on whether that reaction is reasonable or not. In Joyce's case, her assessment was that showing her emotions was not acceptable or in Martin's best interests. I explained to her that the problem now was not that she was upset — the problem was that she was upset with being upset.

Joyce acknowledged all this and then said she feared that if she started to cry she may never stop. I reassured her that she was bound to stop sooner or later. I was right — it only took three days! What happened was that given permission, Joyce's tears began to fall like summer rain — soft, steady and fairly continuous! Once she started, Martin joined in and between them they still hold our record for the most tissues used in a program. In that environment, a residential program with no outside pressures or distractions, and surrounded by others who had a genuine, compassionate understanding of where they were at, Joyce and Martin shared their grief.

At the end of the program, Joyce made a point of thanking the group for providing them with that special space and for supporting them through that time. She said that now she felt as if a huge weight had been lifted from her shoulders. She acknowledged that there may well be times in the future when she would cry again, but never with the same intensity and always with a new-found ease and sense of appropriateness. Joyce told us all that she felt wonderful as now she did not need to waste her energy attempting to contain her feelings. Now she was free to put all her energy into supporting and caring for Martin.

This is acknowledging where you are at, where you are starting from. Once that is done, in the way that works and is complete for you, then you are free to move on. If you have any doubt about how you are going with this issue, it may well be worthwhile to discuss it with a trusted friend or member of the family, or perhaps go to a counsellor to make sure you are travelling well. Do be warned that there is the potential trap of becoming stuck in the painful emotions. What is wanted is full acknowledgment and expression, then to be encouraged in the ability to move on.

Moving on to learn what to do about it all and putting that into practice.

So the next step is to consider what it takes to develop and use Imagery effectively.

CHAPTER 5

THREE PRACTICAL PRINCIPLES

Key criteria for effective Imagery

As was pointed out in the introduction, Imagery techniques can be learnt and applied with little depth of understanding and still they may work. However, the more you do understand what you are doing, why it works and how, the more power you give to it. Having studied and developed the theory behind Imagery in the second Chapter, what can we say about the techniques?

The three essential principles for the effective practise of Imagery are that the images used need to be as much as possible:

(i)   accurate

(ii)   complete

(iii)   accompanied by a strong feeling.

Each of these three principles is essential to the successful practice of Imagery. We are about to investigate what each point really means and will refer back to these essentials as we detail and practise the different forms of Imagery throughout the book.

The point to make here is that many people find that when they do begin Imagery exercises, that there are elements of their images that are inaccurate, incomplete or that do not feel good. This is a particularly important issue in Healing Imagery but is relevant to all aspects of Imagery.

Why this is so is that consciously you may have a clear intention, a clear goal. However, unconsciously you may well have your doubts or fears. Remember that Imagery is the language of the unconscious mind and that in practising Imagery we are activating this part of our being. So it would not be surprising for any negativity to be mirrored in the images we form.

While in one sense this is a worry, particularly if we do not realize the problem, in a more important sense, Imagery provides an excellent opportunity to bring any negativity to conscious awareness, to recognize it, address it and transform it. This is one of the real strengths of Imagery — that it can be used in this highly creative, personally therapeutic way.

So in this Chapter we will examine the positive side of what Imagery would ideally be. Then we will need to look more deeply into the darker side of the *negative* or scary images and learn how we deal with them.

(i)   Effective images need to be accurate

Probably the reason for the images you use being accurate seems obvious enough. The mind functions using Imagery as its language and operates much like a computer. The old garbage in, garbage out principle certainly applies, so that if you give your mind vague, indecisive or inaccurate images to work with, there will be little or no result.

The mind is goal-orientated; it likes clear goals and once it has one, it will do its best to implement that goal, irrespective of whatever type of goal that happens to be. Importantly, the mind does not discriminate when it comes to using Imagery. It will do its best to fulfil a goal whether it be destructive or constructive. The imperative to get it right then, remains with the initiator of the image. Once the image is being used, the mind will support it with the full force of its creative power.

A classic healing example of the need for accuracy involved a young boy with cancer who was having chemotherapy. He was hoping to use the image of two warplanes to empower his treatment. When asked to draw all this, he drew two planes attacking head on, each firing bullets at the other. One plane represented the cancer, the other the treatment. In the drawing, however, when the two lines of bullets were extended, the bullets from the chemotherapy plane missed the cancer plane, while the cancer plane's bullets went directly into the chemotherapy. In other words, the boy was reflecting his inner belief that the cancer was stronger than the chemotherapy, and that he expected the treatment to do little good.

Now I guess that you could go into all sorts of in-depth analysis with all this. However, in my experience all the boy needs is to be told to shoot straight!

While unconscious beliefs can affect the nature of the Images we form, the reverse is also true. Imagery can be used in a highly creative, personally therapeutic way to change deeply held unconscious beliefs. This is an exciting field of therapeutic work and it offers real possibilities for personal development as we will discover soon.

How then can you be sure your images are accurate? One of the best ways is to draw them. You can make just one drawing to represent your Imagery at work; or do what many do and draw a series of 'cartoons' that set out in more detail what your Imagery involves. Then find a counsellor or valued friend you trust. Explain to them what your intention is with your Imagery, then show them the drawing(s) you have made and ask for their feedback. With a trained counsellor this can be a very valuable exercise, while even a perceptive friend is likely to notice any glaring inconsistencies. As the drawing is a reflection of your own state of mind, it is common that initially you may not notice even what, with the benefit of hindsight, seem to have been obvious inaccuracies.

So while being accurate is a key issue in Imagery, these solutions also relate to the next point — that your Imagery needs to be complete.

(ii) Using images that are complete

That the images be complete is another crucial factor which often comes into creative and positive thinking. In my very early days of learning and using these principles, I had a friend Geoff who was even more convinced of these principles than I, and he used Imagery techniques regularly. Geoff was on a real spiritual journey in his life and very deeply committed to living his truth. A business opportunity arose which was highly ethical and which would lead to genuine benefits for many people. To take up this rare opportunity, Geoff needed $10,000! Having been preoccupied with his spiritual life, Geoff had no cash or assets although he was well educated and highly talented. So he had a genuine need and decided to test his principles.

Geoff imagined receiving the $10,000 and affirmed receiving it — using accurate Imagery. (This is a true story.) What happened is that his father died quite suddenly and unexpectedly. In his will, you can probably guess, he left Geoff exactly $10,000 — no more, no less! A remarkable coincidence? No doubt. Quite remarkable! I took the lesson that to be complete often it is wise to add in, almost as a proviso, *'in a harmonious way!'* Perhaps it is being judgmental to suggest that Geoff's father's death was not harmonious. In some ways it perfectly met a genuine need and perhaps it was all as it was meant to be. I know Geoff was deeply disturbed by the 'coincidence' and that it caused both of us a great deal of introspection and reflection.

Another example of this principle of being complete is that I have heard of cancer patients who have used highly aggressive Imagery to attack their cancer. Some have succeeded in becoming cured physically and yet I have been told that some of these people who used aggression have become so aggressive and unpleasant in their own personality that it would be hard to say that real healing took place. To be complete here, the Imagery certainly does need to be accurate and effective in the physical sense. However, it is quite possible to achieve this end while aiming to bring about peace and harmony in the emotional, mental and spiritual spheres as well. These issues will be discussed more fully in Chapters Twelve and Thirteen.

(iii) Empowering Imagery with Feelings

Passion — The driving force behind Imagery

The degree of emotion or feeling, the amount of passion that accompanies Imagery, provides a major key to explain the difference between Imagery that leads to little or no effect, and that which brings about dramatic results. Passion is a high energy state. Passion by definition is a strong emotion which generates enthusiasm and commitment.

It seems clear that active passion drives Imagery!

With passion and its accompanying enthusiasm, there comes determination, resilience and perseverance. With passion all the qualities that lead to goals being fulfilled are present. Also based on recent Mind/Body Medicine research, it seems that passion is a key factor in triggering the changes in brain chemistry that generate both healing and wellbeing.

Passion then, is an essential part of effective Imagery. The only question is what type of passion works best — base passion or altruistic passion?

No doubt everyone can remember having a passion for something in their life. Something you really felt for, loved, were committed to. Something you just naturally were prepared to do whatever it took to achieve. My hope is that you were able to follow it through. Passion fulfilled is a true delight.

Often I work with people who in fairness would say that thwarted passion was behind their illness. Not only am I talking of thwarted love here, although that may well be the issue; but any passion in life that was blocked, put aside, overwhelmed by the busyness of life or just simply put off and forgotten — these are the lost passions that can lead to illness. These are the passions that when remembered and rekindled lead back to life and joy — preventing illness if it has not arrived already, and often sparking radical healing if it is required.

Passion then is a glorious ally in health, healing and wellbeing! But the question remains, what is driving our passion and does it make any difference what is behind these driving forces? Clearly, my own view and experience is that this is a major issue and that we need to differentiate between base passions and altruistic passions.

Altruistic Passion — Compassion

Altruistic passion is the result of a pure motive based upon spiritual clarity. This type of passion is the product of:

Right seeing, Right motive, Right action.

Right seeing is a state where there is a deep wisdom-based understanding of whatever the problem or issues may be.

Right motive is based upon compassion for all, and is a state where there is a commitment to the best outcome for all. Compassion leads to a level of commitment that often has a quality of spiritual devotion. True spiritual devotion is unconditional. It is not a bargain such as 'I will go back to Church if I get the new job!' True devotion is an uncomplicated state of giving your focus to a spiritual reality. While most commonly this occurs in the context of a religious tradition, some are capable of making this commitment in a more abstract way; committing themselves to basic spiritual principles and pursuing a spiritually based life. Pure, heartfelt devotion has a very powerful, very clear energy behind it that empowers all it touches.

Right action is free from the stress of over-reacting or under-reacting, it is simply doing what is required in a focussed, resolute and calmly determined manner. This attitude has the atmosphere of the true martial arts and is a state developed through practices such as meditation, mindfulness and spiritual discipline. It may not be as flamboyant or exciting as the base passions, but there is a calm, an ease and a grace about this state that is heartwarming to be around. It is an incredibly powerful state.

Base Passion

But does the feeling accompanying Imagery need to be so altruistic? Will any strong feeling fire effective Imagery? What of good old fashioned hate, lust, greed and revenge? No doubt we all have our share of those feelings from time to time! Well — not me — but I'm sure everyone else does!! Here is where it gets really interesting and perhaps I have to speculate as research is going on rapidly in this field.

We can all observe the power of negative emotions to fuel personal gain. Looking around there does seem to be plenty of evidence that anger, greed, abuse of power etc. bring short-term gains. Perhaps if physical wealth was the only issue, these emotions would be lauded. Yet looking deeper, the sad human cost of these rampant emotions is heavy indeed.

It is a major tenet of Buddhism that five base passions provide the root cause of suffering: anger, attachment, ignorance, pride and jealousy — all base passions which sooner of later backfire on us at heavy cost. So to heal the heart, to overcome base passions and to aspire to a more altruistic compassionate view, is an essential component of life itself, as well as any truly satisfying and sustaining practice of Imagery. Key practices to assist with this are set out in Chapter Fourteen, Healing the Heart.

The special case of passion in healing

Recent research in Mind/Body Medicine supports my own experience that emotion plays a key role in the mind's ability to activate and direct physical healing. Here again the question — what type of emotion is most effective? Will powerful, fear-based emotions be effective, or are other motives more appropriate? What works best?

In the field of healing, it seems clear that any strong emotion is more beneficial than none; at least in the short or often even medium term.

After our cancer self help groups had been running a few years, we became aware of a dramatic study that was published in the world's foremost medical journal *The Lancet*. This study by Greer and Pettingale[1] investigated the psychological reactions of women diagnosed with breast cancer, and the effect of these reactions on their survival. All the women were found to have reacted in one of four quite different ways. Some reacted with *denial*, pretending as if nothing had happened and attempting to bury their heads in the sand. Others came out with a *fighting* spirit, determined that this illness was not going to beat them and that they would do all possible to become survivors. The next group reacted with *stoic acceptance*, virtually saying 'Why me? Why not! It's here, I guess I just have to put up with it.' Finally there were those who responded with *resignation*, 'Things always go wrong for me, this is just another horrible example!'

After five years the survival rates of the four groups were markedly different. Perhaps, not so surprisingly, the stoic acceptance and resignation groups had fared quite poorly and only 20 per cent were still alive in both groups. Also, perhaps not surprisingly to us at least, the women with a fighting spirit were doing exceptionally well with 80 per cent survival. But there was one big surprise! The women who were using denial also had an 80 per cent survival rate!

At first this really puzzled us. What did it mean? Should we abandon teaching self help techniques like Meditation, Imagery, diet and positive thinking? Should we simply foster denial and discourage people from discussing their problems, sharing their feelings and experiences and actively seeking solutions?

---

1. Greer S. *et al.*, Psychological response to breast cancer: Effect on outcome, *Lancet*, 1979, October, pp. 785–7.

We reflected on this deeply. Then it occurred to me. To react to a major illness such as breast cancer with denial is a very powerful emotional response! Remember that most of these women would have had a breast surgically removed. To carry on as if nothing had happened, to use denial in the face of all that, is a powerful reaction indeed!

So at the time we speculated that these women would not be able to keep it up. Either they would have to change their tactics, or their energy would run out and problems re-emerge.

Another five years later, follow up results were published and again they were quite remarkable. The stoic acceptance and resignation groups had sadly nearly all died. The fighting spirit ladies were virtually all intact with still nearly 80 per cent surviving. But now the denial group had dropped off steadily to 50 per cent. Over the next five years this decline continued to 20 per cent, while the fighting spirit women continued on.

So it may well be that strong emotions, strong reactions of any sort can fire healing in the short to medium term. However, it would seem that it is the life-affirming qualities, that normally we think of as positive thinking and positive emotions, that seem to lead to endurance — as well as happiness!

The fear of death, dying or disease obviously fuels strong emotions and can motivate people highly towards survival. This works well to begin with, and is where most people start. It is a natural response and provides a powerful incentive to get going. However, if fear remains the motivational force, sooner or later it runs out, wears people out, becomes too hard. What does sustain people in the long term is a recognition of the preciousness of life and its wonderful possibilities. To switch from the fear of dying to a joyful, pure passion for life is the key. More of this in the Healing Chapters.

The question of control

A final point to consider is that of the individual's sense of control. Feeling out of control in the normal sense of the word, leads to feelings of hopelessness and helplessness. This undoubtedly blocks Imagery and most other aspects of life. It certainly affects our health dramatically.

A somewhat unkind rat experiment very effectively highlighted the impact of a sense of control. Similar rats were divided into three groups. The fortunate control group were left alone and their lives went on as normally as a laboratory rat's life goes on. The two experimental groups were placed in similar cages with similar conditions. The nasty bit was that the floors of their two cages were electrified. From time to time a mild electric current was switched on. The only way to turn it off was for one of the first group of rats to realize that pressing the magical buzzer in their cage did in fact switch it off. This had the bonus effect of switching off the second group's electric shock as well — only that group did not know how it was all happening. The second group did not have a buzzer, nor could they see the other rats at work. In other words, the first group quickly learnt that the shock came often enough but that they could turn it off. They had a measure of control. The second group had no control. They were subjected to the same amount of electricity, but for them it appeared to occur in a quite random manner that was completely beyond their control!

The outcome? The rats with control had their immune function measured. Initially it dropped, indicating that the stress was depleting them. However, after a while their immune function came up, rose above normal levels and remained elevated! It seemed that being stressed, and then feeling able to overcome the stress, being able to feel in control, actually heightened the immune function of the first group of rats. The second group, the rats with no sense of control, simply died. Quickly.

There is no question that a sense of control is a key factor in health and wellbeing. Again, the question remains — what type of control works?

Phil was what is politely referred to as a *control freak*. An intellectual, domineering type, Phil was highly successful in work and sport. He worked hard, pushed himself, was fastidious with deadlines, always 'on top of things'. Then he developed cancer of the kidney. No problem. Change diet, learn to meditate, use Imagery, even change jobs. Always in control. Tight, rigid, I can do it. I can achieve this.

Then one day Phil woke up and all he could do was cry. No energy. No direction. Just a big black hole ahead, a feeling of emptiness. Phil realised his will had run out. His ego-driven will had run out of push, run out of energy. Phil spent three days in bed in the depths of despair. He felt lost, confused, totally deflated. For Phil it was his 'long night of the soul'; that transformative pit in which all seems lost, until what you are really looking for is found. Phil found his spirit. In the depths of his despair, when all he had been familiar with seemed lost, Phil found his essence — his spiritual essence. And in doing so he found an enthusiasm for life that came from a different place. Gone was the striving of the ego-driven will. In its place was a joyful enthusiasm, a sense of right action, a sense of honouring the sacredness in life by committing all his energy to healing — in body, mind and spirit. This led to a discipline that was easy and sustainable. Phil has become a remarkable long-term survivor.

So it seems that many people these days hope to use ego-based control, relying upon physical, emotional or mental energy. Their hope is to make their world secure. Unfortunately, this means they are placing their hopes for security on things that are inherently insecure — jobs, people, houses, banks. All these things are impermanent. Eventually they come and go. So what does give enduring security? What does give an enduring sense of being in control?

This is the key element of the spiritual path. The recognition of the need to let go of the ego-based sense of control and to put our confidence in a spiritual reality.

There are two options available that will help with this. The first is to build on a secure physical base, to meet our emotional needs and to satisfy our mind. From this security it is possible to launch into the spiritual life. In my experience only a few do it this way. My hope is that more will!

For many, like Phil, this letting go, this transformation, only comes when a trauma or crisis takes us to the edge, to that point where we let go and fly.

My own illness took me past my physical limits; it took me past my emotional and mental limits. In doing so it introduced me directly to the essence of who I really am. This direct experience gave me an unshakable trust in life itself, a joy for it, and a heartfelt commitment to helping others.

So here is another key benefit with Imagery. It provides a powerful way to take back a sense of control. With Imagery you have a means readily at your disposal that you can use and feel in control of. While for many, this control begins with its basis in the mind, we can aspire to higher motives through using the techniques still to come in the Chapters on Invocation, Manifestation and Healing the Heart.

So far we have been dwelling on the principles and basic techniques of Imagery and how to be clear about using them. Now we can get even more practical; discuss and experiment with how to prepare your mind and body to get the best out of Imagery; then we can learn how to practise Imagery for specific purposes.

CHAPTER 6

THE PRELIMINARIES

Preparing for effective Imagery

Having completed some introductory Imagery exercises already, and having dwelt on the theory behind Imagery, you will be getting a taste for what this type of meditative practice is like. Before we go on to delve into more specific applications of Imagery, let us clarify general issues relating to the practice — how to get started, when to do it, how often to do it — how to set it up so that it will work best.

Imagery is a type of meditation practice. To receive the full benefits of this type of inner work it is very helpful to have the broader context gained from understanding the full scope of meditation. So if you have not done so already, I recommend you read my book *Peace of Mind*. This provides an overview of the different types of meditation, a good deal of information on how to begin meditation and in the section on Creative Meditation, quite some detail on Imagery. Then in *Meditation — Pure & Simple*, there is valuable detail on how to relax your body, calm your mind and how to let go into the deeper stillness of profound meditation. While the primary intention of *Meditation — Pure & Simple* is to provide access to the heart and essence of meditation practice, the preliminary sections of this book are specifically relevant as a starting point for Imagery. So do read these too, although I will be summarizing all that is essential for Imagery in this Chapter.

The point to emphasize over and over is that Imagery is a dynamic, willful, mind-generated activity. Imagery harnesses the power of the mind, but as it has been said many times now, Imagery has the potential to be destructive or creative.

One of the surest safeguards for Imagery, one of the most reliable ways to ensure that its positive effects prevail, is to use Imagery against the background of the regular practice of passive, silent meditation. This type of meditation (as described in detail in *Meditation — Pure & Simple*), is essentially aimed at regaining and sustaining a natural state of balance. If we are predominantly in balance, ('predominantly,' because health is regarded as a dynamic state of balance and life is bound to be attended by fluctuations); if we are mostly in balance, then we will find that there are many natural, almost automatic benefits.

The theory here is that when we are basically in a balanced state, many positive qualities find their natural expression. For example, it is natural to be positive, natural to be joyful, natural to be clear and confident. Interestingly, it is also natural to be fearless — babies are born with only two inherent fears — a fear of heights and a fear of loud noises — any other fears we have to learn.

When we relax, let go and return to the natural balance of meditation, we can let go of acquired fears; just as we can let go of tension, anxiety and stress. If we do happen to be stressed, and sadly who is not these days? (unless they have been doing something to let it go already), then we tend to over-react or under-react — neither of which is conducive to confident and effective Imagery practice.

For all these reasons then, it is wise to meditate regularly and to be aware that you are supporting your Imagery in this way.

Given the benefits of passive meditation, where the aim is to calm and still the mind, and given that Imagery very much involves using the mind in an active and dynamic way, many people do ask me which is better, which should I do — Meditation or Imagery? While this is a book on Imagery, I would have to say that for daily, regular practice, if you were only to do one, I would recommend the passive silent form of Meditation. The sustained benefits of a little time spent each day in a state of deep natural balance are profound. However, the Imagery techniques we have been investigating so far and will be discussing and practising further, do have exceptional, specific benefits. So I prefer to think of combining the various practices, keeping the simple Meditation for the regular routine, and using Imagery when the specific needs are there. Many people have benefited from learning a range of Imagery techniques and from having them available for use when required. I heartily recommend this approach!

The Right Attitude

Already, we have discussed in some detail the importance of the attitude with which you approach your Imagery practice. Again, to reiterate, ideally you do Imagery in a state of mind that is clear, confident and calm. It may well be, however, that when you first start a new type of Imagery exercise, or apply Imagery to a new problem or need, you are far from the ideal of being clear, confident and calm! It may well be that the exercise, the Imagery practice that you do, helps in itself to lead you into a more relaxed state where you can regain your sense of ease, and so helping you directly to become more confident.

So, understand that the ideals put forward are just what they are — ideals. Recognize that perfecting any ideal is almost fanciful — yet ideals give a very useful sense of direction. They do point towards what to do, and any step you take towards fulfilling an ideal is well worthwhile. For example, there is no doubt that as an ideal it is recommended to be relaxed. Yet relaxation is not a black and white event — there is a sliding scale from fully tense to fully relaxed. A major principle here is that if you do an exercise that relaxes you seventy per cent, make sure that you delight in being seventy per cent more relaxed than when you started, rather than being stressed by the thirty per cent that you are away from total relaxation.

Be gentle with yourself. But be smart too. So each time you practise Imagery, there are some important preliminaries which will assist you to be well prepared and ready to get full benefit from your efforts.

Preparing for Effective Creative Imagery

1. Prepare your outer environment

Consider what you can do with where you do your practice, so that it supports you best. Ideally minimize all external distractions so that you can concentrate fully on this inner work. Deal with the telephone, take your leave from others in the house.

Ideally use the same place each time for your practice. Make it special with photographs, special objects, flowers and decorations. Many find lighting a candle adds a special atmosphere.

2. Prepare your inner environment

We have spent a good deal of time considering the necessity for effective Imagery of being clear, confident and calm; and how to develop these qualities. Another important attitudinal issue is that most Imagery exercises are done best in a state of open-minded experimentation. While most Imagery exercises are goal orientated and done for a specific purpose, usually with a particular outcome in mind; in an almost paradoxical way, the more open you can be, the less rigid; then the more possibilities can open to you through creative Imagery. This state is really one of positive expectation, which comes free of tension and with a sense of trust in the process and the beneficial outcome. This is another of the things we will discuss specifically with some of the Imagery exercises; it is enough here to mention it and to recommend you to be aware that this open-minded, trusting attitude of experimentation can be very useful.

3. **How often and when to use Imagery**

Some of the exercises you will be learning are recommended to be used as virtually one-off exercises. Others can be used almost daily. Specific recommendations will be given with each exercise.

Many Imagery exercises are quite quick, taking only a few minutes. However, usually the preliminaries take a few minutes and it is often useful before you finish to spend a few minutes relaxing calmly or in meditation before you go on with your day. So most often, ten to twenty minutes is a useful minimum time period, while some Imagery exercises do take longer. Again, specific recommendations will be made as we progress.

As for the ideal time of day for Imagery, there are no definite rules, but you may need to experiment. Most people find that morning sessions are very effective. While some find themselves too sleepy at night, others find Imagery wakes them up and hampers sleep. Some find Imagery at night works well — so you need to experiment to find a balance with your other activities.

A major principle with all meditation practices is that regular practice brings results. For many people a routine helps to maintain the discipline of the practice. Many find a morning shower, followed by Imagery meditation and breakfast, locks the inner work into the daily routine and helps sustain their good intensions.

Going to a group regularly also helps to keep your enthusiasm going — as well as providing continuing input and the benefits of good company!

4. **What position to practise Imagery in**

Most people find that they are more alert in an upright position. While you can use Imagery lying down, there is the tendency to become sleepy, even if you do not completely go to sleep! So, ideally, sit in a chair with an upright back, or learn to sit cross-legged on the floor. An ergonomic chair can give you an excellent posture for meditation and Imagery. There are photographs and more specific detail on meditation positions in *Peace of Mind* (pages 48–54).

5.   The Relaxation Response

This is the ideal technique to prepare you for any type of meditation practice. In its own right, the Relaxation Response has powerful benefits as it provides a reliable means that will help you to relax your body and calm your mind. Just practising this technique regularly will alleviate stress, help you to regain and sustain that natural sense of balance, prevent illness, accelerate healing and leave you feeling a stronger, more enduring sense of peace of mind.

The basics of the Relaxation Response involve learning a method of physical relaxation and then using the principles of concentration and observation to allow the physical relaxation to flow on so that your mind too becomes more relaxed and calm. In this relaxed, calm state, and being aware of all the principles we have discussed already, you will be in an open yet focussed state of mind, ideally prepared for the use of this creative side of meditation.

Happily, the Relaxation Response is an easy exercise to learn and practise. For most people it is quick and satisfying and well worth regular practice. You may have learnt how to do this already but here is a summary of what to do. What is recommended, is that you use this process as a preliminary to any Imagery exercise, as well as taking time as a separate exercise to practise and improve your relaxation skills via learning the Relaxation Response.

For beginners, it is best to approach learning the Relaxation Response in a structured way. Then you can steadily simplify and speed up the process so that eventually it requires little time, but can still be used as a powerful preliminary to other deeper or more involved practices.

Most people find the Progressive Muscle Relaxation exercise (the PMR for short) an ideal, methodical and reliable way to start. To restate what was first set out in *Meditation — Pure & Simple*, beginning with the feet, you work up through each muscle group of the body, contracting and relaxing the muscles. What the exercise does is to focus your attention on each major muscle group in the body. By contracting the muscles you highlight the feeling of tension in that area. Then relaxing the muscles, you have an exaggerated feeling of relaxation in that area. The result is that the muscles are able to let go and become more deeply relaxed than they were to begin with. The effective result is a consciously relaxed body.

With each muscle group then, what is required is to give your full attention to each of the following four feelings:

(a) The feeling of the muscles at rest — what the muscles feel like when you first give them your attention.

(b) The feeling when the muscles are contracting — what the feeling of tension is like.

(c) The feeling of the muscles as they are relaxing — the feeling of letting go. This actually is the feeling of the Relaxation Response.

(d) The feeling of the muscles when they are deeply relaxed.

The way to get the best from this exercise is to give it your full attention — to do it mindfully. To actually contract and relax each muscle group and to focus your attention on noticing the sensations that are produced as you do so. When you do this exercise and do it consciously, it is very reliable!

A good way to begin, is to read the following transcript of the exercise and then do it for yourself. If this is how you do begin, the idea is to talk yourself through it. So read the transcript in italics, then take a few moments to become familiar with contracting and relaxing each muscle group progressively up through the body.

For the exercise itself, say the words quietly to yourself — 'contract the muscles' and 'let them go' — as you actually do the exercise. Then, leaving gaps between each phrase, use the other words and phrases to evoke deeper feelings of relaxation. These other words are deliberately abstract in nature, and aim to avoid analysis or judgement. Their purpose is to help to keep you focussed and to assist in the process of letting go.

Many people find it helpful to link the saying of each phrase with their breathing. This provides a pleasant rhythm to it all and is inherently relaxing in its own right. To do this say 'Contract the muscles' on an in breath, 'And let them go' on the following outbreath.

Then take another whole breath in and out without saying anything. Breathe in again, and on the outbreath, say the next relaxing phrase like 'Letting go', 'Deeply', 'Completely' or whatever else you are using for that purpose.

Learning and practising this approach in a group is obviously helpful as you will have a direct experience of it all. Tapes can be useful if you do not have direct access to a teacher. At home, tapes are of particular benefit because they keep you on track and they help you to develop a gentle rhythm. They remind you to pay attention, they bring your focus back if you do get distracted. Also they avoid you having to think about what to do next, you can just be led by the words and flow with them. Some people, therefore, make their own practice tapes by recording the exercise for themselves. As explained already, I have made specific tapes to complement this particular approach and book.

So here is the exercise:

The Progressive Muscle Relaxation Exercise used as a prelude to Meditation and Imagery

You will find it best to give yourself at least 20 minutes to practise this exercise. This will leave you with some time to be still at the end, just resting with the relaxed feeling you have produced.

So go to your meditation space, take up your position, check your attitude and begin your practice.

Let your eyes close gently ... Turn your thoughts inwards ... And remember that this is a time to bring the mind home ... To relax ... And let go.

Now, really concentrate on your feet ... Perhaps move them a little, really feel what they are like at the moment ... Now, contract the muscles of the feet, feel the tension ... And let them go ... Feel the muscles relaxing ... Feel the muscles becoming soft and loose ... Feel it deeply ... Completely ... More and more ... Letting go ...

The calves ... Contract the muscles, and let them go ... Feel any tension relaxing ... Soft and loose ... Feel it deeply ... It is a good feeling ... A natural feeling ... Feel the letting go ...

The thighs ... Contract the muscles, and let them go ... Feel it all through ... The legs feel warm and heavy ... Soft and loose ... More and more ... Letting go ...

The buttocks ... Contract the muscles, and let them go ... Deeply ... Completely ... Feel it all through the pelvis and around the hips ... Sometimes it helps to imagine a belt or band around the hips has just been loosened a little ... Relaxing ...Releasing ... Simply letting go ...

The tummy ... Contract the muscles, and let them go ... Feel it deeply ... Calm and relaxed ... Calm and relaxed ... Completely ... Feel it all through ... More and more ... Letting go ...

The chest ... Contract the muscles, and let them go ... Feel it all through the chest ... Now, just allow the breath to take up whatever rhythm feels comfortable for you at the moment ... Effortlessly ... Effortlessly ... It is a good feeling ... Feel the letting go ...

The arms ... Contract the muscles, and let them go ... Feel it in the hands particularly ... You might feel a warmth, a tingling flowing into the hands ... Perhaps a lightness ... Almost like they could be floating ... Just going with it ... Simply letting go ...

The shoulders ... Contract the muscles, and let them go ... Feel the shoulders drop a little ... Feel it deeply ... More and more ... Deeper and deeper ... Letting go ...

The jaw ... Contract the muscles, and let them go ... Feel the jaw drop a little ... Feel it deeply ... Calm and relaxed ... The tongue soft and loose ... It is a good feeling ... Feel the letting go ...

And feel it up over the nose and through the cheeks ... Feel it deeply ... Completely ...

Now the eyes ... Contract the muscles, and let them go ...Feel it deeply ... All through the eyes ... Almost like the eyes are floating in their sockets ... The temples soft and loose ...

And feel it around the ears ... The back of the head ... Up over the top of the head ... Calm and relaxed ... Calm and relaxed ... Simply going with it ... Letting go... Simply letting go ...

Now the forehead ... Contract the muscles, and let them go ... Feel the forehead smoothing out ... Calm and relaxed ... Feel it all through ... Through the body and the mind ... Deeply ... Completely ... More and more ... Deeper and deeper ... Letting go ... Effortlessly ... Effortlessly ... Letting go ... Deeply ... Completely ... Letting go ... Letting go ... Letting go ...

Rest quietly now for a few minutes before completing the exercise, perhaps stretching a little, and then letting your eyes gently open again.

This PMR based exercise provides a fairly structured, easy to learn and reliable means of relaxing the body and calming the mind.

What you need to do next, is to learn how to:

1. Simplify the PMR so that you are able to relax more quickly.

2. Practise the PMR in a more thorough way so that you are able to relax more deeply.

Then you combine what you have learnt from these two techniques, so that you can relax quickly and deeply.

There are more complete details of how to do this in *Meditation — Pure & Simple* on pages 86–90 and pages 98–110.

Relaxing more quickly

Briefly, you simplify the PMR in several stages. With each simplification, the aim is to end up with your body just as relaxed as you remember it having become with the practice of the full PMR; only now you get there more quickly.

So, first experiment with and become proficient with being able to relax each muscle group without contracting the muscles. Then combine muscle groups so that you have the sense of relaxing the legs as a whole (rather than feet, then calves, then thighs).

Finally, it can be almost as if you can relax the whole body as one unit. Almost like throwing a relaxation switch! Many people find that this is helped by taking a deeper breath in, then sighing the breath out, feeling almost like a wave of relaxation flowing right down through the body; releasing any tension with it and leaving you feeling calm and relaxed.

Relaxing more thoroughly

The next series of exercises involves spending more time relaxing each part of the body, so that you learn to relax more thoroughly.

You can begin by choosing one big toe. Imagine as if you were travelling through the toe in your mind, feeling the skin relaxing, the tissue under the skin. Feel the muscles relaxing; travel under the nail and feel that area relaxing. Feel it too through the joints, the bones; through every part of the toe. You may even be able to imagine finer detail, almost as if you were relaxing each cell, each atom!

Focussing your attention on the fine detail of relaxation in this way, leads to a profound sense of relaxation. It releases any long-held or deep-seated tension and can be freeing in many remarkable ways. This exercise does take time and con-centration, but it is highly recommended. The more you do it, the more thoroughly your body will relax, and the more familiar you will become with what it feels like to have your body deeply relaxed.

Relaxing quickly and deeply

Remembering that feeling of deep relaxation, now combine it with what you learnt of how to relax quickly. With a little more practice, soon you will be able to put the two together and relax quickly and deeply. Now you have available to you, as an inner resource, an ideal prelude to any Imagery exercise.

However, there is one more major issue to address before we explore the specific applications of Imagery, and that is the question of how to deal with unpleasant, uninvited or even scary images that may occasionally present themselves.

The Uninvited

While for most people the practice of Imagery is beneficial and pleasant, it is not uncommon for uninvited images to come to the fore from time to time. Often these are inconsequential and can be dismissed or let go of, just like the myriad of random thoughts that tend to wander through our minds throughout the day.

However, sometimes images can form that seem to have more moment. Perhaps they have an intensity that surprises you. Perhaps they reflect issues you are worried by or perhaps they are downright scary. Sometimes too it is possible that images form that seem quite malevolent, as if they represent some force intent on doing you harm.

The problem I have in discussing all this, is that I do not want to conjure up for you any negative or scary images! It is a well known fact that what you expect to happen in Imagery, is highly likely to occur. So, I can say that the issues we are discussing now, the appearance of negative or scary images, is not a big factor in the experiences of most of the people I work with. But certainly it is common enough to warrant a forewarning, especially as the techniques to deal with all this are relatively straightforward and often lead to very important benefits in their own right.

As an interesting aside, in many Eastern cultures, where that culture is rich with the notion of good and evil spirits, Imagery can be really exciting! With different expectations, the major issue in Imagery for these people is often how to deal with these more challenging images.

This is certainly an area of inner work where we need to differentiate between 'negative' and 'challenging'. In Western culture, most people instinctively label disturbing or scary images as negative. Certainly they can be very disquieting, especially if they are powerful, as they sometimes can be. You need to be aware that if you plan to meditate long term, or use Imagery regularly, that 'negative' images sooner or later are likely to present themselves. How you respond to them will be a key to your ongoing practice.

For example, Judy was a very active mother of two teenage children who also ran a busy gift shop. She began Meditation desperate to find a way of relaxing and anxious that if she did not do something soon, she would develop a stress related illness. Judy learnt from *Peace of Mind* and then made the effort to get up a little earlier each morning to meditate for twenty minutes. Starting with the PMR and flowing on into simple silence, Judy soon found that it was working; she was coping better all round, feeling more relaxed and happier within herself. Then as she was meditating one day, as if from nowhere, a face appeared in front of her closed eyes. It was strong and clear; the face of her much-loved, but somewhat austere and feared Grandfather. She was quite taken aback. He had been dead several years and the shock and surprise of this image quite upset her. Fearing the face would reappear, and being unsure what to make of it, Judy stopped meditating for many months.

Then, when I was conducting a meditation workshop interstate, Judy came along and during a break, tentatively asked about her experience. I explained that often these apparently scary images could be very helpful and, rather than recoiling from it, she might like to approach it in a sense of enquiry, perhaps even asking her Grandfather why he was there, what he might want or what he had to offer?

In the atmosphere of the workshop, Judy felt reassured enough to let go more deeply again and, perhaps not surprisingly, her Grandfather's face reappeared. This time Judy stayed with the image and asked him what he wanted. He said simply and clearly that he wanted her to know that he was all right and that he was there to help her.

Judy told me of all this at the end of the day. Tears were in her eyes as she attempted to describe the reassurance she felt from this; reassurance that her Grandfather was well, and that his presence was there to support her. Reassurance too that on a grander scale, death had lost something of its sting.

Classically then, these images that come uninvited, are often initially disturbing. However, far more often than not, they can be of great value when we know how to work with them. So what are the possibilities?

Dealing with 'negative' images

There are five options available.

1. **Tell the image to go away**

    (Some people prefer to use more emphatic, more colourful language!)

    This is a useful technique for the minor nuisance type images that tend to be a fairly regular feature of most people's inner life. A specific example would be if you were doing the Quiet Place Imagery as we did for the Inner Wisdom exercise and a snake wandered uninvited into your place of peace and calm, disturbing you and disrupting the tranquillity. You could just remind it whose head it was in anyway, and tell it to go away! This works well for minor issues, although you may prefer to investigate what the snake has to offer in the manner described in (4) below.

2. **Open your eyes and leave the exercise**

    If at any stage you encounter an image that you feel really uncomfortable with, you can be assured that you have the option of simply opening your eyes. The image will disappear and you will be back in the room where you began! You may then prefer to get up, do something else for a while and return to your Meditation or Imagery when you feel more settled.

A strong word of advice here. If you have this happen, it is very important that you tell someone about it. Keeping it to yourself tends to bottle up the fear and energy of the experience; talking about it tends to let it go. So you may tell a family member or confidant, you may seek out a professional counsellor. Often the sharing of these experiences is accompanied by an emotional release, most commonly tears; however, there is bound to be a feeling of relief also and with that a greater capacity to integrate the experience.

If at any stage you do get strong recurring images that disturb you, I strongly recommend that you approach a professional for help. In my experience with the exercises throughout this book, major problems are a very rare occurrence, although many people do have lesser experiences which they can sort out on their own in the ways being described.

3.   **Choose to concentrate on a more pleasant image**

It is hard for the mind to hold two images simultaneously, so another way of dealing with 'negative' images is to use selective concentration and to focus on happier themes. There are many ways you can do it, many other things you could concentrate upon. One obvious way to do that is to recreate in your mind your Quiet Place — that place where you feel particularly peaceful and comfortable. There is more detail on this technique in the next Chapter.

4.   **Let the image run**

By this I mean that rather than telling the image to go away, rejecting it or attempting to change it, you adopt a curious stance and let the image develop. This becomes a bit like watching an internal video clip. So, without trying to influence it, you approach the image like an impartial observer, almost like someone observing an interesting movie, and notice how it proceeds. This may well lead to the disquietening nature of the image becoming more intensified, but often it leads to a dramatic, positive conclusion. If you can stay with the image, sit it out as it were, this is one of the best options. It is worth giving a powerful and dramatic example.

John was a highly stressed, deeply anxious middle level executive. He had a very nervous manner, chronic skin problems, a stomach ulcer and acute shyness. He gave the impression of being permanently embarassed in other people's company and his unease was apparent to all.

John was looking for solutions, but was so anxious and fidgeting that he was one of those rare people who we found was really unable to sit still to meditate.

In a personal session, John was asked to imagine a Quiet Place, a place where he could feel particularly peaceful and comfortable. John struggled to locate such a place and the torment was obvious on his face. Finally he settled on a clearing in the middle of a large pine forest, in the dark of night, with the wind howling and the sense of an impending storm! Some quiet place! But then things seemed to rapidly deteriorate and a very dynamic Imagery sequence unfolded.

John said that at first he felt as if the forest was closing in on him. It seemed as if there was a narrow trail leading away from the clearing, so he headed off down it. All of this was very clear in his mind. He lost all awareness of the real physical surroundings he was in; it was as if all he was describing actually was happening.

As he walked along this dark, narrow and winding path there was the sense of the trees leaning over and moving in to block his way. He felt that the path behind him seemed to be closing in, in a menacing way, and he started to run. The more he ran, the more the trees closed in. He was soon moving at a frantic pace.

Finally, he emerged from the forest only to find himself on the edge of a deep ravine, a wild river raging along way down below him in the gloom. Looking to his right, John noticed a swing bridge but as he approached it he could see it was very old. The ropes it was suspended from were worn and fragile. The wooden slats of the footbridge were decayed and many were missing. With a sense of desperation and the sense of still being pursued, John began to clamber across, some of the slats collapsing under his weight, the bridge groaning and straining. Nearing the other side, the whole structure disintegrated, but he was able to leap at the last minute, catch hold of the bank and scramble up the other side.

This was all sounding like an extraordinary episode from *Indiana Jones*; but for John it was real, intensely real. He was sweating now, talking feverishly as he described what came next. He was confronted by a towering mountain. The only way to proceed appeared to be a narrow path that wound around its base and then headed up. The higher John went, the steeper the cliff face became. Now he was moving around the edge of the mountain and the path he had to walk on was becoming narrower and narrower. In fact the path shrank down to be more like a ledge and John described the steep drop below him, the rocks he could see at the bottom and again the turbulent river tumbling along in the darkness.

But now, impending doom. The ledge itself began to fade. It was as if the ledge began to merge into the rockface ahead and was closing over behind. John was left with less and less to cling to. The fear was real. John felt sure that he was about to fall to his death on the rocks below. The feeling of panic was very strong. Finally, there was nothing left to do. He could only let go.

A remarkable thing happened. John had the feeling of falling a little, a sense of hopeless abandonment; but then, instead of falling further, he flew!

John's whole countenance changed as he said in another voice — a quiet, incredulous, happy voice, 'I'm flying, I'm flying. I can fly!' John felt himself soar like a bird, rising higher, arching gracefully, circling, delighting.

Finishing the exercise, John's face was radiant. It was clear he had had a major experience and that a huge inner transformation had taken place. Given John's history, he did need ongoing support to maintain this new-found freedom and confidence. But he was on the way now, and this Imagery exercise had become a remarkable turning point in his life.

Some people find that just following John's Imagery affects them quite strongly too. We actually have used it as an exercise for some people struggling to overcome fear. It is certainly a dramatic, yet fairly typical example of the benefits that are possible in letting 'negative' images run.

Now be clear — you may find John's experience an interesting exercise that is quite manageable to follow. If, however, your own fears present themselves through Imagery, you too may find them very scary. It does take a good deal of resolve to sit there, feel them and let them run when you are on your own. It can be done, however, and it works very well — especially if you are forewarned and know what to do. There is still another possibility.

5.   **Welcome 'negative' images, communicate with them, and learn from them**

Often as you meditate more, and pursue your own personal development, you come to realize that it is the difficult areas that offer real gold. Often those things that are confronting or scary are those things that we have found difficult, that we were unable to cope with in the past, that we would have preferred to be different, that we do not want to acknowledge as being a part of our own nature, or that we simply have not integrated into our conscious awareness and life. This is the realm of the *shadow* as it is called. It is that part of us that we choose not to face and that we attempt to contain by suppressing in our unconscious. To do this takes ongoing energy, like keeping the lid on a pressure cooker. When we relax and meditate or use Imagery, it is not surprising that the pressure is released and these suppressed images can re-emerge.

Experienced meditators then come to welcome these images, these shadowy elements of their own underworld. They welcome them like old friends, enquire deeply into their nature, treat them with respect, compassion and humour, let them run, investigate them, and then either integrate them into their conscious awareness or release them altogether.

To conclude, what appear to be 'negative' images often enough have purely passing nuisance value and deserve to be released or moved on from in the easiest and most effective way possible.

You will have an obvious sense of when one of these images warrants more attention. The images to work with are the ones that are more intense, more demanding and often quite scary. If you can, use your will to stay with these images, open to them, allowing the accompanying feelings to flow and letting the images run. Sometimes a dialogue will be valuable, often there will be an outcome that may be all of surprising, relieving, instructive and transforming.

The common experience is that when you work with these images effectively, they are truly valuable.

Having now delved into the basic theory and practice of Imagery, and being forearmed with the means to experiment with more specific exercises, let us examine the areas where specific forms of Imagery are most powerful and creative.

CHAPTER 7

INNER PEACE

Imagery for relaxation, stress management and meditation

Travelling interstate by car a few years ago, I was first upon a fairly serious accident. Actually it was a rather beautiful day; clear sky, not a cloud to be seen, early Spring. Not a breath of wind, quite still. There had been a series of sweeping bends dropping down the side of a rather steep hillside, and towards the bottom there were two hairpins. Rounding the second of these very tight curves, I looked across to see a motorbike upended in the ditch; its rider lying flat out beside it. It seems he must have lost control coming through the bend, skidded, bounced into the ditch and stopped rather suddenly.

Having delighted in motorbikes myself in earlier days, and being first on the scene, naturally I went to assist. As I made my way across the road, the deeply distressed moans of the young bike rider became more audible. And the swearing! He was lying on his back, the shirt scraped off his left shoulder, a large gouge out of the side of his helmet. But it was his left leg that was the real problem. He was leaning sideways, grasping the leg above the knee, squeezing it, obviously in great pain. My veterinary training was not necessary to see that below the knee the leg was broken clean through and markedly displaced.

The young man's face was severely distorted. His teeth were clamped firmly shut although his lips were retracted back in a grimace. His eyelids were narrowed while the eyes themselves were almost jumping out of his head, like those of a frightened animal. His forehead was deeply furrowed and as I approached there was a mixture of distress, pain, pleading and relief.

Sitting down beside him, I asked him his name. 'Steve,' he groaned. It seemed apparent that apart from the leg, any other injuries were only minor. Soon other people stopped and one went off to call an ambulance. Steve asked me what had happened, how his leg was, and for some help to get his helmet off. I judged it to be the right thing at the time to reassure him with the truth. There was the sense that he thought the leg to be grossly mangled. So I explained that the leg did have an obvious, but clean break. I gave him my opinion that it appeared to be the sort of break that would heal well and quickly. I told him that help was on its way and that an ambulance should be here soon.

Then I asked Steve if he wanted some help to relax. It was all he could do to give a rather pathetic nod of his head. So I asked Steve where his favourite place in the country was. He looked puzzled; it was painful for him to do anything including speaking it seemed; but I asked him again — in a quiet even tone.

Steve told me that there was this place down by the beach that he liked to go. As it happened, this was a beach that I was familiar with and I asked him to describe to me what it was like the last time he was there. What time of day had it been?

Late afternoon.

What was there to see there? Steve said that he liked to sit on a particularly rocky outcrop and look out across the sea to a medium sized island where he knew seals lived. What was the sea like?

It was fairly calm with only a small swell running.

As he described the place more, Steve started to relax a little. I suggested to him that he might like to close his eyes and imagine he was back at that place while he described it a little more to me. He seemed to sense the possibility and immediately closed his eyes. What sort of a day was it?

Clear sky, light breeze, only a few clouds.

What was the beach itself like?

There is (Steve was talking in the present tense now) *a sweeping sand beach, around a wide bay.*

What colour is the sand?

Very white, well just a hint of yellow.

And what is at the end of the beach?

It rises up to quite a high bluff.

What is on the land?

It's almost completely clear; the grass is short and mostly brown, only a few trees here and there.

So what sounds can you hear in this place Steve?

There are a few birds calling behind me, off to the right, they sound like magpies.

What about off in the distance?

I can just hear the sound of the waves.

What about smells, can you smell anything here?

Well, there is the smell of the grass; it's a bit like it's just been cut. And there is the salty smell of the sea. It smells really fresh.

By now Steve's face was showing definite signs of relief. The tension was going, the distorted lines smoothing out. His breathing was slowing too, becoming a little deeper and the distress in his voice was giving way to a quieter calm.

So what temperature is it Steve? Is it warm, or cool, or neutral?

Well, it's early spring so it is warm but there is still a bit of a bite in the air.

So what about the rocks you are on, how do they feel?

Well they are warm too, but hard.

And how does the sun feel upon your skin?

Well, it is warming; it feels good.

So what is the overall feeling for you being in this place Steve?

Well, it feels really good. It's the place I come to when I want to get away from it all, when I want time to myself, to think a bit, to just look out at the sea.

And if you were going to lie down and rest for a few moments Steve, where would be the best place to do that?

Oh, there is this grassy patch just behind the rocks. It's protected from the wind and the sun shines right down on it.

So why don't you go there now Steve, and as you do, lie down. As you lie down, feel your body relaxing, in fact feel it relaxing so much that you feel almost as if you are floating up off the ground a little. Just rest there now, feeling almost as if you are floating a few inches up off the ground.

All this conversation had taken place with Steve lying in the ditch, me sitting by his head, one hand on his head, the other on his arm. Despite quite a crowd gathering and the predictable consternation, we were able to focus on Steve's Quiet Place. The more he seemed to recreate his favourite beach in his mind, the more he seemed to relax, to be oblivious to his obvious predicament.

It was not long before the wail of the ambulance could be heard off in the distance. Steve was carefully loaded onto a stretcher and was soon speeding towards professional care.

The experience reinforced for me the power of Imagery. When the mind is focussed in this way it can provide exceptional First Aid as it disassociates from a painful, unpleasant experience and becomes absorbed in something far more pleasant. This is a great technique to use in an emergency, or at times of acute distress. As it did for Steve, it can provide rapid relief from both physical or psychological pain, help restore a degree of calm, and create a situation where whatever the real issues are, they can be addressed in a more effective way.

This then is an example of how Imagery can be used to create a place of inner peace and how it can be very effective, despite starting amidst major pain and distress.

Many people find this same technique to be very helpful as a lead-in for their daily meditation. Having relaxed physically, this type of Quiet Place Imagery can be a useful intermediary step that helps make the transition from a busy mind to a quieter, more peaceful state. For some, this Quiet Place becomes almost like an Inner Refuge, a Sanctuary into which they can retreat to get away from the bustle and pressures of daily life.

This sense of having an Inner Refuge can be useful in another way — as an aid in pain management. Especially for short-term pain, such as for a short surgical or diagnostic procedure, you could close your eyes, relax a little and then imagine yourself in your Quiet Place. Some people find that this works particularly well for them. It is as if they can disassociate their attention from their body for a while, by focusing their attention elsewhere and imagining that they really are in their Quiet Place. Then, once the procedure is completed, they bring their attention back to their body.

In all these contexts — first aid, meditation and pain relief — the principle that explains how the Imagery works is by association. By imagining a place that you associate with feeling calm and peaceful, you immediately begin to feel more calm, more peaceful.

So there are a few steps to follow to develop this exercise more fully. You need to build up the details of your Quiet Place. Focus your attention as you generate and really *feel* all the sensations that are involved in your experience of your Quiet Place. At the same time, the more you become immersed in the feeling of this place, the more it seems as if you are really there, and the better it works.

There is a preferred order to all this which focuses attention on each of the senses in the order that is easiest for most people.

The Principles for creating the 'Quiet Place'

Pay attention in turn to each of the following senses, taking time to build them up as fully in your mind as you can:

1. *The visuals:* What can you see? Notice what is nearby, in the middle-ground and off in the distance. Notice any movement, what time of day it is, if the sky is visible and clear, or cloudy. Notice the shapes and sizes of everything, e.g. if there are trees, are they short or tall, are the trunks fat or thin; what shape are the leaves, etc? Notice too the colours, paying close attention to the shades or variations in colour.

2. *The sounds:* What can you hear? Listen for what might be close by. What sounds are coming from further afield?

3. *The smells:* What can you smell? Notice what fragrance or odour there is in this place.

4. *The physical sensations:* What do you feel? What temperature is it? Is there any wind on your skin or sun on your face? What does it feel like? What do you have contact with? Is it hard or soft, damp or dry, warm, cool or neutral?

5. *The tastes:* What can you taste? Often in this Quiet Place Exercise taste is irrelevant, but it may be an issue if say you were in the sea and could taste the salty water.

6. *The feelings:* How does it feel to be in this place? The feelings are very important in empowering Imagery, so really dwell on the good feeling that goes with your Quiet Place.

7. *Any changes:* Remember that if there is anything that would make this place even more peaceful or comfortable, then you could change it.

Most people who try this exercise feel that it works reasonably well. Some find it exceptionally helpful, some a non-event. About three-quarters of people in my experience find it fairly easy to see their Quiet Place and to *feel* as if they are really there.

Others notice that the pictures seem rather vague, indistinct or fuzzy. This need not be a problem unless it concerns you! It is that sense of being in the place, and having a strong association with the place via the feelings that seem to make it work best for most people. However, if your visual Imagery is not particularly clear to begin with, most people do find that it improves with practice.

For a written introduction to the Quiet Place Imagery Exercise you can refer back to sections 2 to 5 and 7 to 8 on pages 43 to 45.

There is another style of using this same principle on my tape *Guided Imagery.* The Healing Journey is an Imagery exercise that involves archetypal symbols of letting go, cleansing, healing, regeneration, new beginnings, relaxation and meditation. Used regularly, such exercises can bring about sustainable changes and a heightened sense of inner peace and wellbeing.

Imagery for Deepening Relaxation

The next useful way to consider using Imagery is as a means for deepening relaxation, particularly for the letting go of long-held or deeply-ingrained tension. For most people, practising the Progressive Muscle Relaxation Exercise (PMR) has the effect of relaxing the body fairly thoroughly. However, having completed the PMR, if you scan your attention through your body again, you may well find that while most of the body is reasonably well relaxed, there are some areas that still feel tense, tight or even painful. These areas will feel different from the rest of the body. Usually the feeling that goes with tension or pain, is one of feeling hard, denser than the rest of the body, contracted, isolated. Sometimes these areas will be hotter, occasionally cooler; but always, when you really focus your attention upon them, they feel obviously tenser, or more painful than the rest of the body, and certainly different.

This feeling of being different to the rest of the body is a key to noticing areas that need to relax more. You can help them to relax consciously in a number of ways. Repeating the whole PMR is one way. Simply letting go more, feeling the body relaxing, that sense of the Relaxation Response flowing more, can do it for some. Imagery is another way. This can work very well using the White Light Imagery (see pages 137–149) or the Mindfulness for Pain Relief techniques (see *Peace of Mind*, pages 177–180). These are major healing techniques, however, they can be used just as well for physical relaxation and as a lead into Meditation.

Imagery and Emotional Expression

Another potentially powerful way to use the principles of association and Imagery, for relaxation and emotional ease is by using the technique described by Manfred Clines in his book *Sentics*. The basic intention of this exercise is to spend two minutes each on a series of emotions, generating one at a time, one after the other. While the book goes into some detail with all this, I have found that many people benefit from using the sequence in its simple form — just allowing the feelings and images to come up as you think of each particular emotional state.

You will find that you can probably do this just reading words from the book. If you choose to try this, I do sugg you do it at a time when you have some space to yoursel afterwards and preferably at a time when you have a member of the family or a good friend around. This is because some people find that just bringing to mind these emotional states can have a stronger impact than expected and you can get stuck for a while with the feeling. The intention, however, is to feel each emotional state for just two minutes and then to move on.

So go to the place where you normally practise your meditation or Imagery, or you can do this exercise just sitting in a chair. Using the words as triggers, dwell on the *feeling* that goes with each emotional state. Build that feeling as strongly as possible, give it two minutes, and then move to the next.

It can be a good idea to simply sit for a few minutes at the end of the exercise before you move off again. So here is the sequence:

The Emotional States of the Sentic Cycle

1. No emotion.
2. Anger
3. Hate.
4. Grief.
5. Love.
6. Sex.
7. Joy.
8. Reverence.

Notice how easy or difficult it was to evoke each emotional state. What images accompanied the feelings? How easy was

...n and move on to the next? Did you get ...motions? How do you feel now? Are ...e of the emotions conjured up by this ... you let them all go and move on unaffected?

... this exercise regularly can build a flexibility with emo-tions that can enhance the freedom of emotional expression. This can be accompanied by a calmer, easier state of mind and the more appropriate and open flow of emotions in daily life. If you sense it to be helpful, there is a benefit in doing the exercise daily for some time.

There is some similarity in this exercise to that of Inner Rehearsal — the next major area of Imagery where we learn how to practise doing things in our mind with the intention of improving our performance.

CHAPTER 8

INNER REHEARSAL

The key to improved performance

Betty was a keen golfer who happened to have breast cancer. She was a spritely sixty year old who had a good deal of vigour as well as sporting grey hair and the wisdom of years. For Betty, the golf was more important than the cancer. Club competitions were the highlight of her week and she practised regularly.

The bane of Betty's life turned out to be her slice. She viewed the cancer as a significant but relatively minor annoyance; something she felt she could deal with. Betty became an enthusiastic member of our Support Group where the conversations over cups of tea invariably revolved around golf — and the slice. It seemed that Betty had a long history with this slice. It had become a regular part of her game since she took up golf for exercise in her early fifties. Ten years later, Betty was delighted that her general play continued to improve steadily with her years, while her frustration mounted as the slice seemed to become more deeply entrenched. Many lessons had been devoted to the slice, many hours of practise focussed on correcting this basic flaw in technique. It seemed that the more she practised, the more Betty practised her slice — as a slice, it got better and better!

Salvation came in the form of a top International golfer. He joined the Group to learn how to deal with his cancer, and in the wonderful way that synchronicity works, he sat next to Betty.

During the discussions in Imagery in the Group, we were exploring the role of Inner Rehearsal — how it is possible to practise an event in your head, to practise it perfectly and condition yourself to improve the outcome. Our golfing friend really warmed to all this. He explained how he spent about half his golfing practice time on the fairway and half in his armchair at home. He explained that the joy of practising in your head is that you can do it there perfectly! Once you learn what the ideal swing looks like, it is possible to rehearse it in your head as if you actually are doing it. He explained that he was able to do some of this Inner Rehearsal as if he was in his body actually hitting the ball. He would imagine all types of shots — from the tee, fairway, rough, bunker, on the green — and practise them in his head. Sometimes he would 'watch' himself hitting the ball and he had the ability to see himself from any angle, making corrections, perfecting his technique.

The point is that swinging a golf club to hit a golf ball is an automatic action. It involves such a complex sequence of muscular activity that it is controlled by the automatic, unconscious part of the brain. We have the conscious thought, 'I will hit the ball,' but when it comes to the doing of it, the message must be relayed to that automatic part of the brain which sets it all in motion.

Now, for the action to be able to be performed, that automatic part of the brain has to learn what to do. Hitting a golf ball is not a natural instinctual thing. While we may have a natural skill or aptitude, we still need to learn. It is almost as if the automatic part of the brain that controls golfing technique needs to be programmed. This is done in part via conscious learning and input, but for most people the majority of the learning happens through the repetition of physical practice. So those early lessons, the early experiences, are key events that lay the foundation for future development.

In Betty's case, her slice became programmed, encoded, very early in her golfing career. The more she practised, the more she practised her slice, the more deeply entrenched it became.

As our golfing expert continued to explain what he was doing, Betty's eyes lit up. Her whole demeanour lifted to a new level of vitality — she was excited! We talked more about the method of Inner Rehearsal after the group and Betty could not wait to get started. She figured that if she did this inner work and practised a slice-free swing, she could finally rid herself of her problem. From all her reading and lessons she was now so familiar with what to do, now she felt that she had a workable solution.

Betty found the practice came easily to her. Each morning and evening she consciously relaxed her body and went through the Relaxation Response. In that calmer, more peaceful state, with clear resolve she imagined herself following through with the perfect swing. She could see it, she could feel it. She watched the ball sailing down the middle of the fairway.

Later that year a very excited Betty returned for our Christmas celebrations. After ten years of being in the middle order, Betty had just won the Club annual competition! She was so delighted, it was as if the cancer was a non-event. She was so full of enthusiasm for her golf, so pleased with the demonstration of what her mind could do with the golf, that she remained fully confident of staying well and living joyfully.

Another friend who works in this field took up skiing later in life. His children had been pressing him and his wife for a few years, the enthusiasm was sustained, so James decided to join in. Being aware of the potential of Inner Rehearsal techniques, James began his skiing during the summer — in his head! Watching videos, reading books, talking with friends who skied, James became familiar with skiing styles. Each day he relaxed, cleared his mind and then went skiing!

James did most of his Inner Rehearsal as if he was in his body actually skiing. So he imagined clear sunny days and the snow fields sloping down before him. He felt the bite of the cool winter breeze, tempered by the warmth of the sunshine and the thick comfort of his ski pants and parka. He felt his hands in their thick gloves grip his stocks, he felt his feet held firm in their boots and binders. Then he imagined the freedom of the skiing. He decided to rehearse parallel skiing and felt the exhilaration of the turns as he watched his progress down the slope — steady and flowing.

With Winter, the sense of anticipation to head for the snow was strong. The children, who had been a trifle sceptical of Dad's inner games, struggled in the beginner's group. Meanwhile, Dad sailed off, doing in reality the smooth parallel turns his mind was now so familiar with! A few lessons anchored his technique and skiing became an instant delight.

Inner Rehearsal is a mental technique that nearly all elite athletes appear to use — either because they (most likely) do it naturally, or because they have learnt how to practise it. Inner Rehearsal has been demonstrated to significantly improve the accuracy of free throw shooting in major league basketballers. It provides a powerful key to improving any sporting performance. As a technique it is easy to learn and you are bound to notice its benefits.

The necessary steps to improve performance using Inner Rehearsal

1.   Understand the theory

As in all Imagery exercises, the more you believe in what you are doing, the better it will work. So take time to appreciate the simple links between the conscious thought (wanting to perform better), knowing what better (or best) really is, and the fact that performance is largely controlled by the automatic, unconscious part of the brain. Appreciate that by conditioning the brain's automatic control centre for your sport, you can program yourself for improved performance.

2. Clarify the ideal

Obviously if you are programming yourself, you need to program the best possible pattern. So talk with your coaches and your peers, read the books, watch the videos. Whenever you can, see the experts live and study how they do it. It can be helpful to imagine yourself almost in their skin, emphasizing the feeling of what they are doing and how they feel themselves. Form a clear image of the ideal.

3. Relax prior to Imagery

Use the standard preparation recommended for Imagery exercises. Give yourself time and space, clarify your intention, relax physically, calm your mind — use the principles and techniques of the Relaxation Response.

4. Practise Inner Rehearsal

Imagine yourself performing your sport in an ideal manner. This manner needs to be within the realms of possibility — for you. So imagine the best that you can be and practise that. If you are a fairly short teenager then imagining yourself slam dunking like Steven Jordan is a good goal to work towards in the more distant future, but this is a separate exercise to rehearsing what you are capable of right now. So for current performance, for example, in the terms of a season you may be just starting, imagine the best performance you can for that time frame. It is fine to be a little fanciful in pushing the limit of what your best may be. Be fully optimistic! For this technique to work, however, you do need to be able to believe that your goal, your ideal is possible. Practising a performance which you feel is beyond your reach, that is impossible for you, will not work.

Remember too that this technique certainly can be used in stages. So you can imagine your performance improving to a particular level for now, do the sport, experience your 'live' performance improving and then use this newly gained confidence as a base to extend your goal towards even better results.

When it comes to the actual Inner Rehearsal technique, there are various ways to do it. You can quite safely experiment with these to find out what works best. In my experience, the guiding principles are that your Imagery is accurate and complete and that whatever you do feels good to you.

Having said that, if it works, it probably is the ideal to practise most of your Inner Rehearsal as if you are in your body actually doing the event. The more senses you can engage in the process the better. So what do you see, hear, smell, taste, touch (feel) as you do it? The more of each sense (that is relevant) that you can activate and build into the Imagery, the better. Also the feeling that goes with all this is critical. Again the ideal is to feel calm, assured, confident, joyful, successful. Some people find it easier and more effective to watch themselves perform — almost like watching a video of themselves in action, while some almost talk themselves through the rehearsal (remember Debbie Flintoff-King). Most people find one of the techniques is easiest for them, most benefit from doing a little of each.

5.. Wherever possible, leave some time at the end of your Imagery to sit quietly — either simply resting or taking a few minutes to enter into meditation.

For most, Inner Rehearsal is a straightforward technique that is both fun and rewarding to practise. Remember the section in Chapter Six on problem solving if any difficulties arise; otherwise may good luck and better performances be with you!

Now of course this same technique can be used to improve other performances beside those in sport. Andrew was a successful Real Estate Agent whose success was built on his ability to talk with people. He was genuinely interested in what his clients wanted, was very personable and liked by many. Unfortunately for Andrew, his ease with speaking with individuals and small family or business groups, did not extent to larger scale public speaking.

As a result of his spectacular sales figures, Andrew was invited to speak at a National Sales Convention. While honoured, Andrew was terrified. The prospect of performing in this way filled him with dread and his anxiety was high.

Andrew approached me thinking that relaxation may be the key. I explained to him that probably this would be a good part of the solution, and then we discussed Imagery. Andrew was very confident of what to say in his speech. He had a reflective side to his nature and quite some Insight. So he really had something worthwhile to offer. I reinforced this for him and reminded him that his audience would be hoping to learn something from him, that he had 'the goods' as it were, and would satisfy them well. We discussed the old trick of imagining an imposing audience as if they were all seated in front of you in their underwear! Andrew really enjoyed this Imagery, the humour helping to put him at ease a little.

Once Andrew had learnt to relax more thoroughly and to practise basic meditation, we had a base to work from. I instructed Andrew to begin his Inner Rehearsal practice with the Relaxation Response. Once he was feeling calm, he was to imagine the hall he would be speaking in and the audience gathered in their seats. He could imagine the atmosphere that went with the other speakers and then imagine his time was approaching. If at any point in the exercise, he became nervous, felt anxious or uneasy, he was to leave the image and return to the peace and calm that went with the Relaxation Response. Andrew found it easy to re-establish his own sense of calm by letting go and meditating, while some other people actually use the Image of their Quiet Place (from the previous Chapter) as the sanctuary from which they foray into this type of Inner Rehearsal.

The first time Andrew imagined himself being introduced and walking onto the stage, his pulse raised, he felt as if he would break out in a sweat and butterflies churned in his stomach. He stayed with it as long as he could bear it, then let the image go, relaxed and re-entered that peaceful calm of his meditation. As he relaxed, he felt his tension drain away, his body relax, his breathing deepen. Staying with this calm feeling for a few minutes, he then was able to imagine walking onto the stage maintaining some degree of calmness. This time he was able to begin his speech, running it half way through in his mind before the fear rose up and unsettled him once more. Letting go, relaxing, back to the meditation. Settling, adjusting, integrating. With the next run through a little more progress, a growing sense of ease and confidence, the realisation that it was working, that a change was possible, the start of buoyant optimism.

With a few more sessions, Andrew could rehearse his speech thoroughly and comfortably in his mind. He concluded the exercise by imagining the audience applauding and friends congratulating him after the event. Next I suggested that he imagine himself several weeks after the Convention. Andrew was to look back on the program, feeling satisfied with his performance. Then he was to imagine the feeling of looking forward to his next opportunity to speak.

Happily, all this did work exceptionally well. Andrew admitted to being a little surprised by how much positive feedback he received and how in fact he actually did enjoy giving the talk!

This same process also can work well for changing phobic patterns. First establish a safe inner place where you can be filled with feelings of peace and calm. From this base, this sanctuary, you can do as Andrew did for his speaking, then imagine the thing that scares you, whether it be spiders, open spaces, flying.

Imagine this thing in a way, and at a distance, that you can manage.

With spiders as the example, perhaps the best you can do to begin with is to imagine a spider locked up in a jar that is in a house some distance away! The idea is that you then imagine moving progressively closer to the spider. Whenever, if ever, you feel anxiety or fear rising unmanageably, retreat to your inner sanctuary, reestablish your peace and calm and then return to the Imagery.

This simple Imagery exercise has helped many people who were determined enough to persevere with the technique. Once you have established a basic level of comfort, in a controlled situation, you then imagine coming across the problem suddenly, reacting quickly if needed, but calmly in whatever for you is a reasoned and comfortable manner.

This same process has been helpful for many people involved with healing. Whether it is using Imagery to accelerate healing by rehearsing an ideal outcome, or learning to reprogram conditioned nausea with chemotherapy, there are many possibilities to detail in the Mind/Body Medicine section coming up.

As a natural extension of this Inner Rehearsal technique, what we will consider next is how we can use Imagery to reprogram old habits — how we can let go of old, unwanted patterns of behaviour and how we can use Imagery to establish new ways of doing things.

CHAPTER 9

THE POWER OF THE MIND – I

Changing habits, realizing your goals

Simon was a highly successful Insurance salesman who came to one of our first Inward Bound programs. This program developed from the realisation that the success of our more specific cancer self-help programs lay in the fact that what was helping people to heal was that we were able to help them to live well. The four key principles in the program — good diet, a positive state of mind, meditation and an effective support network — seemed to reliably transform illness into health and wellbeing. However, we soon realized that while it was wonderful to help people to overcome illness and regain health, it would be even better to prevent illness in the first place. Even more, there was the possibility to play a part in helping people to maximize their potentials and to experience a high and sustainable level of peace of mind.

So Simon joined the Inward Bound to learn to meditate, to reconsider his lifestyle in general and to take some time for personal introspection. What surfaced quite quickly was that Simon really did not like his job. Sure he was good at it, very good. Sure it paid his bills. Paid them well, gave him security and many choices. But no real happiness. Simon loved people. He loved to help people, and he realized that he wanted to be of more help than selling insurance. Simon also realized that he did love the business world. He enjoyed being with people, working with people. Actually, he really liked the bustle of city life but became aware that with insurance work, he was working on his own most of the time. Simon decided it was time for a change.

Reflecting on what he really wanted to do, and what he enjoyed, Simon decided that human relations management met all his work criteria. Simon enrolled in a part-time Psychology degree and re-entered the world of active study. It was a major effort to maintain his family life, his competition squash and to keep his insurance work going to pay the bills. My guess is that often enough Simon would have felt the pressure and perhaps grumbled a bit with the load. However, there was never any hint of giving up, never any waver in his resolve. At the same time, Simon did not need to practise Affirmations and Imagery to do all this. His mind was made up, he was determined, he was embarking on a new career. And he did.

I imagine that we can all recall episodes like this in our own lives. Times where we were so clear, so determined to do something, to achieve some particular goal, that nothing could stop us. We simply pushed on in an uncompromising way, made whatever sacrifices were necessary, did whatever it took, and fulfilled our goal. *And* enjoyed doing it!

Then again, I can also imagine that most of us have suffered from *New Year's Resolution Syndrome*. You know the one — this year I am going to give up smoking! Or this year I will exercise every day! Or this year I will transform my anger. These good intentions make so much sense! They are logical choices, obviously in our best interests. Everyone around us it seems would welcome and support the changes. It should be so easy! Yet how often does it seem that only a week into January and rather than enjoying having made the changes, there is that nagging, recurrent guilt of not even being able to remember exactly what the resolution was!

A little while ago, I was talking to an old friend Margaret. She was telling me how everything in her life was going so well. Her children were all doing well at school, things seemed to be just delightful with her husband and what was really amazing her was how successful her business was. It seemed that work was flooding in so fast that what had been a struggling florist shop was rapidly becoming a secure enterprise.

As we were parting, Margaret threw away an extraordinary line, 'You know Ian, it's all too good to be true!' It's all too good to be true! Margaret was voicing her inner belief. Too good to be true! When I saw her again a few months later, her expectations were back to normal. There was discord in the house, the flush of business had evaporated and she was living the struggle again.

I have another remarkable athletics story. The last of the decathlon's ten events is the 1500 metres. The other nine events revolve around speed and strength, so most decathletes struggle with the longer, endurance based 1500 metres. This was certainly the case for me. At the end of the best competition I ever had at the National titles, I was approaching the bell lap, the last lap of the 1500. I was feeling terrific! I was moving easily, unexpectedly easily for me, and I felt as if I could really go on with it. Then as the bell sounded, I heard the lap times being called. I was thirty seconds ahead of my best ever time! Thirty seconds!! An extraordinary thing happened. Within about fifty metres every joint in my body was aching, my muscles tired badly and soon I had slowed to a crawl. Struggling across the finish line, my time was just two seconds lower than my previous best — I had almost finished on time! In retrospect, I often wonder what would have happened if I had not heard that lap time. I suspect I would have discovered that I was capable of running much faster than I had always thought I could!

It must be easy for each of us to reflect on times when goals seemed easy to achieve, other times when we seemed content (in a funny sort of way) to give up all too easily and soon. We can notice how the mind restricts us, often binds us to old patterns, and notice too those magical times when the mind sets us free.

The question is, does all this happen at random or can we have some control. What would help us to find and sustain real happiness?

Clearly this is where the mind plays an active and dominant role. What the mind believes in, accepts as possible and targets onto, will greatly affect our lives and the lives of those around us. In this Chapter then, the aim is to look a little more deeply into what is happening when the mind works well, to learn the principles behind mind power and to investigate how we can apply them.

The specific areas we will consider are how to achieve goals in uncertain areas where our initial commitment may be faltering, how to change unwanted habits and develop more effective life patterns, and how to develop and sustain positive emotions.

The first thing to observe is that these are all natural functions. We are all positive thinkers to some degree; we all achieve some of our goals, some of the time. The question simply is — does this happen often enough, effectively enough, powerfully enough, to meet our needs?

Given that all these 'positive' qualities, these life-affirming qualities are basic, natural functions and given that we can all observe them working quite effortlessly in our lives some of the time; we need to consider first what would help this to happen more often. It seems that when all these positive factors are flowing easily in our lives, there is a clarity, a confidence, a simple but uncompromising dedication to the goal, that is quite effortless. These qualities are in themselves, reflections of a state of mind. It is a state that seems free of doubt and uncertainty, a state that will not be put off, a state that has this clear conviction of purpose.

While this clear state of mind can come to us almost as a gift in some situations, the most reliable way to develop and sustain it is through meditation. Terry is typical of the many business people I meet who start to meditate. He was telling me recently how much his confidence has improved since he began to meditate regularly. As well as feeling more relaxed and calm, he said how decisions just seem to be easier to make, easier to commit to, and how the choices he is making seem to be turning out really well for him.

Meditation then is a key to Positive Thinking. The more often and the more deeply you enter into the simple silence of profound meditation, the more you return to that natural state of balance, then the more it seems you connect with your own Inner Wisdom and all it has to offer. This is another reason to recommend that you maintain a regular practice of meditation.

Now some people say that meditation is all you need. Meditate and your natural positivity will emerge. You will know what to do, make the right choices, follow through effectively. Meditate and positive emotions will flow naturally. You will be more open to love — to receiving and giving in a joyful way. Meditate and all will be well.

I would really love to be able to say that it is as simple as that. To some degree it is — to *some* degree! There is no doubt that meditation has profound benefits and that it does bring out much of the best in us. For some people the positive benefits and changes that meditation brings into their lives, are nothing short of spectacular. However, I have to say that in my experience, most people need some active work to overcome old mind patterns, old conditioning, old beliefs, old ingrained habits.

This then is where positive thinking and mind power exercises are well worth learning and practising. While there may well be other approaches that help change our old ways of thinking, our old habits, Affirmations and Imagery are dynamic and reliable techniques that have worked for many people.

As we have found in other sections of this book, when it comes to changing habits and achieving your goals through the use of Affirmations and Imagery, the first step ideally is to build a framework of understanding. Affirmations and Imagery are the techniques that utilize the remarkable creative power of the mind. As a recurring theme, the more we understand how these techniques work, the more we believe in them, the more effective they will be. So what follows is a summary, there being more detail in the Chapters on Creative Meditation in *Peace of Mind*.

Essentially the key issue here is the major role that beliefs play in determining our thoughts and actions.

We have a fundamental commitment to act in accordance with our beliefs. When we are doing what we believe in, we feel comfortable, satisfied. We have peace of mind. When our actions do not match our beliefs, we feel uncomfortable, we have a deep sense that something is wrong and we become highly motivated to do something about it. So what we believe in becomes a yardstick for our actions. For constantly we are striving to fulfil our beliefs, to live true to our beliefs.

Given this, what we happen to believe in takes on a huge significance. While it would be ideal if our beliefs reflected a fundamental truth, it may well be that the beliefs we develop are the reflection of the whole range of our life experiences and result in both positive and negative expectations.

If you say 'This is too good to be true' or 'That always happens to me' or 'That is not like me to have done ...,' then you are voicing an inner belief, a reflection of your attitudes.

These beliefs will be a product of either direct or secondhand experiences. Secondhand in the sense that we learn from the experiences of others, what we read or see on film. Direct experiences involve our own perception — what we take to be real experiences. While much direct experience is valuable, it can be quite limiting. Our perception relies upon our five senses — what we can see, hear, taste, smell and touch — as well as our more intuitive faculties. Even with sight, which most of us rely upon so heavily, we know that we see only a narrow band of the light spectrum. For example, if we did have a slightly wider range of sight, we would see with X-ray vision — and what a different world we would live in! However, importantly what we perceive, we generally take as being real. If this perception is inaccurate and it concerns a major life issue, we could develop an inaccurate belief that affects our life in a major way.

Julia was a very likeable lady. Her outgoing personality had led her into a successful designing career but her personal life was dogged by emotional distress, and she had cancer! At one of our residential programs she spoke of how many relationships she had been in, with what appeared to her to be highly suitable men. Yet time after time, the relationships turned sour. Julia realized that she had a huge problem with allowing intimacy into her life, that she had barriers up to deepening relationships. She realized that relationship breakdowns had not 'just happened'. In fact more often than not she had actively destroyed them by the way she acted.

Then Julia made the connection. As a young girl she had grown up in the country amidst a large family. There seemed to have been much of the best of country life — close contact with nature, an easy lifestyle, lots of friends and time with her parents and extended family. Then at the age of seven, Julia had been diagnosed with measles. In the family's large farmhouse the only place that Julia could be isolated was in the rather large pantry. Julia went from living in the midst of a very large, open, loving family, to being confined in an internal room with no windows, poor ventilation and quite a few rats! She wondered what she had done wrong. Her seven year old brain concluded that she must have been very bad, that no-one really loved her, that she was not even worthy of love! In retrospect, as an adult, Julia knows that her family really did love her, but this one powerful childhood experience overrode all that and was anchored deep inside.

Also, as an adult, Julia was driven to succeed and in doing so was able at least on one level to prove some self worth to herself. However, Julia came to realize that her deeply held belief of being unworthy of love had sabotaged all her relationships. What she needed was to change her inner belief.

Now the real secrets behind all this. Beliefs themselves are made up of images that are stored in the unconscious realm of our mind. As we know already, through the use of Imagery we can communicate with our inner world, so with Affirmations and Imagery we have direct access to effectively changing, developing or sustaining our beliefs.

For example, Betty was a senior lady whose life had been lived helping others. She had supported her husband in his work, raised a fine family and contributed to her community. But now she had cancer with secondary spread, and in medical terms, a hopeless prognosis. But Betty loved life and felt she had more to do. She came to our groups with her rather reluctant, but duty-bound husband. Philip took all the sessions in, while he remained somewhat distant and aloof. Betty's condition appeared to deteriorate at first, her pain became worse and despondency set in. Sitting in her armchair one evening, tears began to well up in her eyes. Philip, sensing Betty's mood, asked her what was wrong. She spoke gently of how perhaps it was all too much, perhaps she should face reality, accept her fate and give up on getting well. Now, as it turned out, up until now, Betty had always been a rather negative person. She explained later that a string of events early in life had not worked out as she hoped, she had taken those experiences in and developed a pessimistic view. She had come to believe that things always went wrong for her.

But at the groups, Philip had been paying attention. He had taken in the discussion of beliefs, Affirmations and Imagery, and he knew that Betty was working on becoming more positive with the Affirmation 'I am a positive person now!' So

Philip said to his wife, 'That's strange. What are you now?' 'What do you mean?' responded Betty rather gloomily. 'Oh, I thought you were a *positive* person now.'

Betty told me later that this was a magical moment in her amazing recovery. With her husband's words, it was as if some inner switch was thrown. 'Yes' she said, 'You're right. I *am* a positive person now!' From that moment on, Betty's focus was on the positive side of life. Instead of the old half empty glasses she had been dealing with, now she truly saw the glass half full. She looked for the positive aspect in every situation, found it and found a wonderful inner peace. Her physical recovery was quite remarkable and over ten years later her calm and joyful manner is a delight to all who know her.

Here then is a summary of the basic theory regarding how beliefs develop — and how we can change them if we choose.

1. We have a range of life experiences which we take in consciously via our five senses.

2. These experiences are stored in the unconscious realms of the brain as memories.

3. Memories are made up of images — primarily pictures, sounds (words) and feelings. Tastes and smell can be involved to a lesser degree.

4. The emotions that accompany memories have a big bearing on how important they are to us. The more dramatic (strong) the emotions, the more prominent the memories, and the greater their impact in forming beliefs.

5. Memories accumulate to produce beliefs.

6. We have a deep-seated commitment to act in accordance with our beliefs.

7. For the purpose of these exercises, the unconscious mind cannot distinguish between a real life experience (and

the set of images that go with it) and ones we generate (through the use of Affirmation and Imagery).

8.   We can use the techniques of Affirmation and Imagery to establish, change or reinforce beliefs in a way that they will be effectively anchored and responded to.

The strong suggestion is to spend time reflecting on these principles. Study the section in *Peace of Mind* (pages 147–197). The more you understand all this, the more you contemplate and take to heart how it all works, the easier it will be to use the techniques and the better they will work.

Once you have this solid framework of understanding, move on to put it all into practice.

CHAPTER 10

THE POWER OF THE MIND — II

Affirmations and Imagery in Practice

One of the delightful things about Affirmations and Imagery is that they are rather simple to use. And they work! By following a fairly easy number of steps, you can develop a practice that has the potential to bring major benefits into your life. Again the more you reinforce your practice with a good understanding, the more clarity you have with what to do, the better it all works.

Using Affirmations and Imagery: The 7 Key Steps

1. Acknowledge where you are at — is there a problem, if so, what is it?

2. Set a clear goal.

3. Develop Affirmations and Imagery exercises to reinforce the goal.

4. Practise the Affirmations and Imagery.

5. Support your practice —respond to feedback.

6. Deal with any setbacks.

7. Establish your goal as a part of your ongoing life. Aim to live more fully in the moment.

1.   Acknowledge where you are at

This key part of true positive thinking was detailed in Chapter Four. If a difficulty or trauma in your life has caused you distress, fear or despair, remember that you still do have the choice as to how you respond to that situation. While from the outside no-one could criticize you or blame you for becoming or feeling depressed, is that what will work best for you? Are you prepared to put up with it?

Often a key step in moving forward is to deeply acknowledge what seems to be a problem by allowing the feelings that go with the problem, expressing how you feel to other people you value, you get it out of your system a little, and you are then ready to move on.

You may choose to re-examine the problem in a more positive light. What can you learn from it, what will change for the better as a result of this initial difficulty, how will you and those around you, grow through the experience? So, how can you view this problem as a challenge or an opportunity? What meaning or purpose can you find in it all?

There have been literally hundreds, it may well be thousands of people, who I have worked with that have experienced cancer in this way. Robert is a typical example. A high powered accountant involved in management takeovers and restructuring, Robert admitted to being a tough number cruncher. He hardly knew his children, fought regularly with his wife and, despite material success, was deeply unhappy. His cancer diagnosis was devastating. He had the sense of impending doom and that the happiness he had hoped he would always find, was going to elude him. He rapidly plunged into the depths of despair and strong suicidal thoughts filled his mind.

Amidst this depression Robert came to our groups and realized there was hope. He leapt at the possibilities and with his usual flair, vigour and commitment, proceeded to turn his life around. He changed his attitude, he changed his lifestyle, he changed his job. His health changed and he became another to experience a medically unexpected and quite remarkable recovery.

These days, Robert thanks the cancer for what it has done for him. Like so many others, he says that it was as if, before his diagnosis, he was living his life on automatic, putting up with so many compromises in his life and hoping that some time off in the future he might find happiness, might have time to be happy. The cancer changed all that. With the diagnosis, his future became uncertain, he had to address what was happening now. The compromises became unacceptable, he realized the value of relationships, he set about healing the relationship with his wife and began getting to know his children better. He sought work where he could live his real ethics and sense of values. He thanks the cancer for helping him to reassess his priorities and putting them in order.

It is an unhappy observation that for most of us it takes a major trauma before we deeply question our priorities. So often it seems that we take life for granted, put up with the compromises and hope to find happiness later. Perhaps this is one of the great gifts on offer from the many people I have worked with who have had cancer. Why wait? Why put it off? Life is so precious. And so uncertain. Why not take time now to re-consider what you really value, what your true priorities are?

The 'What If?' exercise

There is a wonderful exercise you can do to help with this. Give yourself time and space and sit down with pen and paper. Fantasize, imagine that for the next three months, everything in your life will stay the same. You will have all the same possibilities, all the same limitations. At the end of this time, your life (your life alone) will end. There is no bargaining, no extension. This is a fantasy exercise and the question is:

If you had three months to live, what would be the ten most important things that you would do?

Take your time to contemplate this question. Then write your answers down. Review them, perhaps you can rank them in order of priority.

The second part to the exercise is to consider how much of your time currently is being given to these priorities? If you are like many people, you may well find that the top priorities are getting very little time. Commonly, they are being put off. So, the question is, 'What would it take to get them done?'

This exercise, done with diligence, can give you the benefits many people get from a life threatening illness, without you having to get sick! It is highly recommended.

Returning to the issue of acknowledging the problem, do all you can to develop a trust in life itself. Trust that there is a meaning and purpose behind it all. Look for that meaning, look for the lesson, the opportunity and delve deeply into the purpose.

With that alone, the goals may well emerge.

2.   Set a clear goal

Goal setting has been given so much attention as it is the crucial step. With a clear goal and a goal that you can trust, and with the confidence and commitment that comes with that clear goal, the rest follows fairly easily. So refer back to Chapter Three to re-examine the goal setting techniques already detailed.

When considering specific issues of personal change, however, there is another process that I have developed that has helped many people to get their goals clear. This has provided real insight into the 'New Year's Resolution Syndrome' and has helped many people to actually bring change into their lives.

It is highly recommended that you do take the time to do this exercise in detail. You will need a pen and some blank paper. If you do use one, record the exercise in your diary or journal.

Personal transformation — A nine step process

I. *Identify the problem*

Yes, you can call it a challenge or an opportunity, but at this stage if it was not a problem you probably would not be bothering with it — so what is it? It could be an issue of physical health, a relationship issue, feelings of low self esteem, work problems, whatever is difficult in your life right now. As an example, I will use an issue from a recent group: Anne's inability to say 'no'.

The first step then is to write on your paper: I. *Identify the problem* — in Anne's case, 'Inability to say no.'

II. *List the disadvantages of the problem.*

In other words, why is this thing a difficulty for you? What don't you like about it? So Anne wrote:

— Always doing things for other people.

— No time for myself.

— Get tired.

— People expect a lot of me and keep asking more of me.

— It's hard trying to guess all the time what others want.

— I end up doing things I don't really want to do.

Make your own list, taking time to reflect, think deeply and be as thorough as possible.

Now, this is where I make the assumption that most people are sane. If you had a problem that was one hundred per cent a problem in your life, and if it had no benefits, and if you were sane, my guess is that you would not put up with it. You would do all you could to change it.

So if you have a problem that is in your life, and that effectively you are putting up with at the moment, my guess is that it has to have some benefits attached. So the next task:

III. *List the advantages of the problem*

In other words, how does this problem help you? How do you benefit from it? What secondary gain might there be with this problem?

For Anne it was fairly easy to come up with quite a list.

— I get lots of good feedback.

— People like me because I am so helpful.

— I feel needed, I feel as if I am being helpful and doing worthwhile things.

As Anne thought deeper, some core issues developed.

— By doing everything for everyone else, I don't have time to dwell on myself. I don't have to face myself.

— My happiness is bound up in other people's approval.

— I don't have to think what to do for myself, other people tell me what to do.

— I don't feel responsible for me; I just do what others want.

For Anne, the exercise was already bringing some revelations!

IV. *Identify the Solution*

At this stage, we are not concerned with how to achieve the solution, how to bring it into reality. That will come later. What we want here is an ideal solution, the best one that you can believe is possible (even if you have real doubts at the moment with how to do it.)

What would it be like if the problem was fixed and you had the ideal solution established in your life. The aim here is to begin to create an Affirmation — a short statement of an ideal, expressed in the first person, present tense, as if it is already done. So it will be, 'I am ...' or 'I have ...' or 'I do ... '. Usually it is: 'I am ...'.

Anne had to reflect on this for some time and discussed it with her husband Jack and our group. The main criteria for Affirmations are the same as for Imagery — they need to be accurate, complete and feel good.

Anne's first attempt was 'I say no.' She really struggled with this. For her, it did not feel good! For me it was incomplete. Obviously there are plenty of occasions where saying 'Yes' is completely appropriate.

'I say Yes or No depending upon the circumstances.' was Anne's next attempt. Knowing her deeply ingrained pattern, I could easily imagine her thinking most circumstances still justified saying 'Yes,' so this was not the answer either.

Anne reflected more deeply on the real nature of the problem. She came to realize that her real issue was self worth. In the past she had not valued herself enough to say 'No.' She had let all her boundaries down, given all her energy away and was allowing other people to live her life for her. She decided that it was time to take her power back, to reaffirm her self worth, and to begin living her own life once more.

Anne's next affirmation was 'I am worthy of love.' For Anne, this meant that she would love herself enough to respect her own needs. She would recognize what she could do for others and be comfortable with her limits. She would recognize when people were honouring her and her talents and asking her for help out of that respect. To be worthy of love, Anne knew she would have to re-establish her boundaries and feel better within herself. She was optimistic with the possibility but certainly fragile. The next steps highlighted all this.

V.   *List the advantages of the solution*

This is usually easy enough and obvious enough. Anne's list (for the advantages of being worthy of love):

— I will feel good.

— I will have more control over my life.

— I will be able to say no when I need to and have more time to myself.

— Relationships will probably become more genuine.

Now again, presuming we are sane, my guess is that if you had a solution that was one hundred per cent advantageous, you would be so strongly drawn to it that you would have taken it up long ago. If this is not the case, then it is a reasonable proposition that there are some disadvantages to the solution. The next step then is to enquire into what these disadvantages might be.

VI.   *List the disadvantages of the solution*

Some of these may be apparent but often you have to reflect rather deeply to get to some of the core issues. For Anne, the list was very revealing:

— People might not like me if I say 'No.'

— People may think I have become selfish.

— I actually like doing things for other people.

— How will my husband react? (It is worth stating here that Jack was a very big man, quite charismatic and very dominant. It was easy to imagine that he enjoyed having a wife who said 'Yes' to all his demands, just as it was easy to imagine that for Anne it would actually be easier to say 'Yes.')

— It would be difficult to change; I am not sure if I could do it even if I wanted to. (This brought out the fear of failure — a common obstacle that limits the goals people set.)

You will probably be noticing that what this exercise is doing is bringing our awareness more completely to the situation. It helps us to observe both sides of the problem and the solution. It is really an exercise in mindfulness and understanding. With this, solutions and right action become more obvious and easier to follow.

VII. *Choose between the Problem and the Solution*

This exercise tends to polarize the Problem and the Solution, making the choice more obvious. It becomes clear, if it was not already, that you can really only do one or the other. So, faced with a Problem with disadvantages and advantages, and a Solution with advantages and disadvantages, which do you choose? Which will work better for you?

People do not always choose the Solution. I remember well Jennifer who came to an Inward Bound program where we did this exercise. She was basically well but happened to have asthma and used it as the focus for the exercise. Once she had considered how the asthma affected her and what was involved in the solution, Jennifer decided to stick with the problem! She decided to simply accept that she had asthma, that that was the way it was, in some ways it was a bit inconvenient, but she accepted it as the best option for now. A remarkable thing happened. Without anything else changing in an apparent way, the asthma went away! It seemed for Jennifer, with this deep recognition, (*not* resignation please observe!) and acceptance, that the underlying problem of her asthma cleared.

For Anne, however, like most people, the solution was far more appealing and she moved on to the next step.

VIII. *How could I sabotage this goal?*

This always seems a necessary step to consider as it is what we tend to do! Besides, it is usually fun to investigate the possibilities, especially in a large group setting! So do take the time to identify what might be the sort of tricks you could use to sabotage your new goal and to help you return to your old patterns? With this knowledge you will be forewarned, notice when traps are approaching and be able to offset them. Anne had a delightful list:

— Put it off, say I am too busy to make the changes just yet, but I will do it later.

— Forget to do it!

— Hang out with all the most demanding people I know so that it seems impossible.

— Don't tell anyone I am trying to change, so I am not too accountable.

— Do it a few times, but focus on feeling so bad about it, that I give it away.

— Worry about how Fred will react.

— Not take any risks.

Being aware of the potential hazards helps to accentuate the need to reinforce the changes.

IX. *How could I reinforce this goal?*

This brings out all the means available for using the power of the mind and how to reinforce our good intentions. Before we consider this in detail, let me finish Anne's story.

Anne left the program all fired up for change. The mouse was ready to roar! I could not help admitting to some apprehension myself. If Anne did manage to make these changes, to assert herself, and learn to say 'No,' how would the dominant Jack respond? Several months later I met Jack again. He was so happy. He was genuinely thrilled by the changes that had taken place within Anne. He said, 'At last I have a true partner. While in many ways it was easier when she was so compliant, our relationship was very one-sided. We are both adjusting to more equality and for me it is wonderful.' In retrospect, Jack's changes were probably as amazing as Anne's. There is no doubt he created the space into which she could change and this points to a key principle in making personal change — having good support.

So let us now consider in more detail how to develop and reinforce your goals.

3. How to develop Affirmations and Imagery

Drawing on the details from *Peace of Mind*.

i) How to develop Affirmations

(a) The three essential points:

For Affirmations to be effective they must be expressed:

— in the first person,

— in the present tense, and must be

— goal orientated.

This is a personalized process, something we do for ourself, hence most Affirmations begin with 'I am' or 'I have', etc. Present time is the only time that the unconscious responds to, therefore Affirmations should indicate that the goal is already achieved or reached. The aim is to give the mind a target that it can lock on to — the target is the end goal, hence, 'I am a positive person *now*'.

Other guidelines for affirmations.

(b)   Be positive

Indicate what is needed, not what is not. The mind is goal orientated, it locks on to targets. It needs a positive direction to aim for, not something to avoid. So, rather than saying 'I am not a negative person now' as an Affirmation, use 'I am a positive person now'.

(c)   Do not make comparisons

There is no need to say, 'I am as good as ...'. Your potential may be to be better, or it may be to be worse. Aim to develop Affirmations that encourage the development of your full potential.

(d)   Unless essential, do not specify a time for completion

As with comparisons, specifying time may slow you down or frustrate you. Part of the joy in using Affirmations is that they release the power of our creativity and Inner Wisdom. The fact is that this part of our being has a wonderful talent for getting us in the right place at the right time — if we just leave it free to do so.

If, however, you have observed your behaviour and find that you are regularly late, and you choose to change that, then certainly consider something like: 'I arrive on time for all appointments, content and at ease'.

(e)   Do be specific, accurate and accountable

The mind needs a specific target. The more precise the goal, the greater its clarity, and the more confident you can be of success.

(f)   Be realistic

You will be limited by what you believe is possible. It is normal to expect some reaction to using Affirmations. 'I am a positive person now', you say. 'No, you're not,' comes that little doubting echo. That is normal. The echo is the old belief having its say. If it were not there, there would be very little need to use the Affirmation in the first place. Remember that this process directs or redirects the mind's attention and mobilizes all its power and creativity. This is a process for making change, for replacing one belief with another, as well as simply establishing a new belief or goal. So do not be surprised by the echo. As long as the Affirmation has more certainty, more expectation, more hope, more *oomph* than the echo, and is repeated, it will gradually replace it and soon become the guiding force.

However, you will need to stay within the bounds of what you can believe is reasonably possible. Do not aim for perfection first off! Be gentle with yourself and gradually set increasingly higher standards and goals.

(g)   Set ongoing goals

This follows on from what was just said. As you see yourself nearing completion of one goal, look for what comes next. Extend your planning and make new resolves.

(h)   Use Action Words and add a sense of excitement

The feeling that goes with an Affirmation has a lot to do with how quickly it will Imprint and be accepted by the unconscious. Affirmations, therefore, work better when said with zest and excitement. One way to do this is to add 'Wow!' on the end of them: 'I am a positive person now — Wow!' Saying 'Wow!' encapsulates that positive, expectant feeling. If 'Wow!' does not suit you, use another word or phrase from your own vocabulary to enliven your Affirmation.

Similarly, look for ways of expressing confidence, ease, naturalness and joy in all you aim for.

(i)   Be precise with the use of your words

Words used in Affirmations are definitely words of power. Pay great attention to how they might be interpreted. You can cover your bets by adding words like 'in a harmonious way.' Be as clear and precise as possible, consider all angles and choose your words wisely. Meditating and contemplating upon your choice of Affirmations before you use them is an excellent way to check their meaning and their validity — for you.

(j)   Keep a balance

Affirmations can have a profound effect upon your direction in life. Consider again the range of goals you are setting. Take heed of your physical, emotional, mental and spiritual needs and those of your family, friends and community. Affirmations are exciting tools to use. Aim to maintain that sense of balance.

Some sample Affirmations for personal development

These are some favourite Affirmations which can act as a guide for your own needs:

(a)   For health

'Every day in every way I am getting better and better'.

This is one of the oldest and most famous Affirmations. It was first used by the Frenchman, Emile Coué, in his book *Self-Mastery through Conscious Autosuggestion*. It remains an extremely powerful and effective tool for mobilizing our inner drive towards better health.

(b)   For relationships

'I greet this person with Love.'

(c)   For self-esteem

'I am worthy of being here.'

'I am worthy of being happy.'

'I am worthy of being loved.'

Before discussing the finer practical details of how to combine the practical use of Affirmations, Imagery and Feelings, let us now look at how to develop Imagery.

ii)   How to develop Imagery

While Affirmations supply the words, Imagery is the use of inner pictures to imprint a new goal on our subconscious mind and so to stimulate our motivation and creativity to achieve that goal.

There are three classifications for the types of Images we can use — Literal, Symbolic, and Abstract.

Literal Images

Here the aim is to see an image of the behaviour, event, or goal literally, the way you are aiming for it to happen. This type of imagery is very practical and can be applied in any situation where there is a clear understanding of the goal.

This approach is widely used in sport. We discussed this technique in detail in Chapter Eight.

Similarly, if you have a very tangible goal like giving up smoking, Creative Imagery can be a great asset. Imagine yourself in situations where you used to smoke, only now you see yourself calm and relaxed, not smoking, and feeling a sense of pride and achievement. Combining this with an Affirmation such as, 'I am a happy, clean-mouthed non-smoker' virtually assures a change in the behaviour.

This is the method of Inner Rehearsal using Imagery and it is an extremely useful and practical technique.

Limitations of Literal Imagery and the use of Symbolic and Abstract Imagery

While literal images are highly effective in sports and for making personal changes, they are often found wanting when you are faced with a complex situation and where your knowledge of the process required to achieve a given goal is unclear. When the goal is clear, but the mechanism for achieving it is uncertain, highly complex or to do with healing, symbolic or abstract Imagery is often far more appropriate.

Symbols can be used to become the vehicle that conveys the conscious intention into the subconscious in a way that the intention can be recognised and acted upon.

Take healing for example. The complexity and timing of the healing process is beyond most, if not all, conscious minds. However, one does not need sophisticated instruments to learn how to influence the body's healing directly. Creative Imagery in either the Symbolic or Abstract form is probably the most powerful tool for this purpose. As we have discussed before, Imagery establishes a link between the conscious intention — 'I want to heal!' — and the subconscious function — How the body regulates its healing mechanisms. We will investigate how these techniques can be used for healing in the Mind/Body Medicine Chapters.

4.   How to Practise Affirmations and Imagery

Affirmations are best said with positive expectation, with power, confidence, and good feeling. If you can do this immediately, you will only need to repeat them for a minute or two a few times a day and they will soon become established. When you have a more challenging belief to establish, you will need to practise more often and for longer periods.

Imagery to go with Affirmations is used similarly — the time depending on the ease and clarity of using the image. Abstract Imagery can be used for longer times, the White Light Imagery, for instance, can easily occupy thirty to sixty minutes. Abstract Imagery makes an excellent prelude to letting go into the simple silence of deeper meditation.

When we combine the use of Affirmations, Imagery and Feelings, we can establish a consciously chosen goal as an anchored belief. This belief will then act as a target which the mind will do all possible to direct us towards.

This process which is called Imprinting, is most successful when there is a close connection between the conscious and the unconscious. This is naturally so when we are in that reverie state just after awaking and just on going to sleep. This, then, is an excellent time to practise Affirmations and Imagery.

Also, singing, or joking with Affirmations loosens the power of the conscious mind and its conditioned responses, and so facilitates the Imprinting process. Making up jingles for your Affirmations, and singing them out loud, therefore can be useful.

Looking directly into your eyes in a mirror and saying your Affirmations out loud with power and conviction is extremely effective if you can do it.

Best of all is to combine Imagery with your Meditation. The meditation provides a poise and balance and has a stabilizing effect on the whole process.

A good sequence then is:

(a) Sit in a slightly uncomfortable, symmetrical position.

(b) Relax physically, inducing the Relaxation Response wherever possible.

(c) Then begin your Imagery.
You can use Affirmations, Imagery and Feelings as a combined approach. This is the most direct and effective way. Sometimes it may seem more appropriate to use Affirmations or Imagery on their own. This may be when an Affirmation is being used to change an undesired state of mind of long standing. Beginning with, say, 'I am worthy of love now', may be best done as an Affirmation at first, moving on to adding Images once some confidence in the accuracy and reality of the Affirmation is

established. Similarly, many healing situations appear to respond well to the direct use of Imagery.

(d) Let go of the Imagery and rest in the natural peace and stillness of meditation before finishing the session.

5. Support your practice, respond to feedback

Reinforce your good intentions with positive thinking principles:

* Develop a support network. Discuss your goals with family and friends. Get them *on side.*

* Seek out allies who can support you actively. Avoid those who challenge you too directly.

* Read books, listen to tapes, attend workshops that support your goals.

* Attend a support group or meditation group that is relevant to your needs. e.g. it may have been useful for Anne to go to a Self Esteem program.

* Tell others of your goal — be accountable.

* Be prepared for setbacks. Changing habits can take time. Be prepared to persevere.

* Be gentle on yourself. Determine to be patient and reward yourself as you notice progress.

* Do seek feedback. Be prepared to reassess your situation, make adjustments and move on.

* Smile regularly! It needs to be fun to be sustained. Enjoy being alive. Change is a feature of life. If you were not changing you would be dead. Enjoy the changes, celebrate your successes. Enjoy!

6. Dealing with setbacks

While it may be that you move steadily and uneventfully towards your goals, it may also be that life goes up and down a little along the way. Setbacks can cause you to reassess your whole situation, strengthen your resolve and lead to useful modifications and changes.

The best insurance against disappointment is to give whatever you do your best. To do everything to one hundred per cent of your ability. Then if you have a setback, there will be no regrets, no guilt, no wondering 'What if ...,' or 'if only I had ...'. At least you will have the comfort of knowing you have been giving it your all. Then there will be a level of acceptance and acknowledgment that leaves you free from looking backwards. You will be free to look forward for fresh solutions.

With this approach, answers to questions seem to come very reliably. When I was ill, often the answers to setbacks came via books. So often, faced with another setback (there were many in my own road to recovery), it would seem as if I was drawn almost magnetically to a particular book. I would open it and there would be the answer on the page in front of me! Often too, old friends would appear unannounced or ring unexpectedly. We would start talking and they would have the answers. The more I trusted in the process, whenever a question or problem presented itself, the more I expected an answer and the more rapidly it appeared. Synchronicity at work! Or is it Manifestation?

7. Establish your goal — move towards the moment

While your new goal and the changes that go with it are bound to require your conscious effort to begin with, it is to be hoped that after a while it becomes effortless. A natural part of your life. As a part of this natural flow be prepared to move on from using active Creative Imagery techniques into the quieter stillness of Meditation.

Be prepared for new qualities in your Imagery and Meditation.

As time goes on, your practice of Creative Imagery will develop and your quality of Meditation will improve. You may discover that this leads to your feeling more in tune with your life and the world around you. You will move steadily into a better experience of current time. You may well find that there is then less need to practise Imagery, that the process of goal setting and achievement begins to flow naturally and easily, and powerfully, with your passage through life.

CHAPTER 11

INVOCATION, MANIFESTATION AND IMAGERY

Linking spirit, consciousness and matter

Manifestation, to make manifest, literally means 'to make obvious to the eye or mind.'

Invocation literally means 'to call upon God in prayer.'

So many people I meet these days are struggling with the conflict they feel between the very real demands and allures of materialism, and their deeper yearnings to expand their spirituality. Many it seems, solve this conflict with busyness. By keeping busy with work, the household, entertainments, travel etc., they block out any real consideration of what life is all about, why they are here (on this planet, in this body) and where they are really going (not just tomorrow but after they die).

Paul Gauguin, that great Impressionist painter said:

'Life is barely more than a fleeting moment
So little time to prepare oneself for eternity.'

Alexander the Great conquered more land and ruled over more of the world than anyone in recorded history. Yet it is said that when he died, he requested that he be wrapped in a simple shroud and that his hands be left out for all to see. They were placed by his side, palms up, fingers outstretched. Alexander the Great wanted to demonstrate to his people what material possessions he was able to take with him!

Many people then, perhaps most even, have a knowing that the material world offers only fleeting delights. Many are seeking something of more substance. Many are seeking an experience of some spiritual reality, hoping for something more direct and satisfying, hoping to find a way to combine their spirituality with their daily life.

Yet for many there is a cynicism to overcome, a disillusionment with the formal religion they might have grown up with, or with spiritual leaders who have abused their powers. For others there is a confusion to deal with as they struggle to integrate the suffering they see all around them with the notion of a benevolent God that appears to allow such injustices.

It seems that for many people in the modern world, learnt spirituality has limited value. Reading the books, being taught dryly at school or in church, only helps to a limited degree. Knowledge acquired in this second-hand way does provide inspiration, direction and some inkling of what is available. But doubts are likely to remain. The only thing that is fully satisfying, and that reliably brings total conviction, is *direct experience*.

If you were able to have a direct experience of a spiritual reality, all doubts would cease. Certainty would prevail. With direct experience comes a knowing, a knowing that is unshakable, a knowing that will sustain you throughout life and through death.

Therefore, in my opinion, of all the benefits Imagery has to offer, the greatest is the very real possibility of it serving to introduce you directly to profound spiritual experience.

Imagery can act as a link between Spirit, Consciousness and Matter.

Imagery provides a very real vehicle for activating your spiritual life, empowering this spirituality with direct experience.

In this Chapter, two major practices will be introduced — Invocation through the use of the White Light Imagery exercise, and the practice of Manifestation. In Chapter Thirteen on Healing the Heart we will develop these themes further with more specific practices.

Invocation and the White Light Imagery Exercise

The White Light Imagery exercise is a core practice for developing your spirituality. Also, it is a key practice for energizing your system, and for healing. In essence, it is a simple practice, perhaps that is why it is so profound. Most people find it easy to use, it is safe and very reliable. I recommend this practice for frequent and regular use. It is particularly beneficial if you are just beginning to use Meditation and Imagery as it has such a wonderful balancing and stabilizing effect.

As with simple meditation, when you practise White Light Imagery it will build a stable base which both empowers and positively focuses other inner work. With time, the practice simply becomes clearer and more potent. I have been using this practice for over twenty years and continue to delight in the benefits I feel from it and rejoice in what it has offered to others who have learnt it. Importantly, I acknowledge the teachings and traditions of the great Tibetan Lama, Sogyal Rinpoche who has been a wonderful teacher for me and whose book *The Tibetan Book of Living and Dying* adds greatly to what I am presenting here rather simply.

There are two main forms of the White Light Imagery exercise that we use regularly. You may find one particularly appealing and concentrate upon that, or you may use either depending on the occasion.

Both these techniques use the same basic principles, however, the first technique makes a feature of using the breath. This means that it requires good concentration and is a little more wilful in its practice. The second technique's approach is based on the quality of Radiant Energy and uses a more natural sense of energy flow. This has a more passive, gentler style. Both techniques are highly effective and I recommend you experiment and decide which suits you best — it may be you use both as many people do. What follows is an outline of the common principles of the techniques, then I will detail how to practise the two variations of the technique.

White Light Imagery — The Principles

1. As if it was in the sky above you, establish an image that represents whatever truth you hold most dear. This can be in the form of a personal embodiment such as a figure that represents God, Christ, Mother Mary, the Buddha or a favourite Saint. You may prefer a more abstract image and use the image of radiant light like a sun shining in the sky above you.

2. Focus all your attention — mind, heart and soul — on this image, and feel its presence. It needs to represent loving kindness, truth, wisdom and compassion. You need to feel that it has your best interests at heart. Build these feelings as strongly as you can, aiming to feel them all through your body, mind and soul.

3. Pray from the depths of your being that all your negativity is cleared, released, let go of, transformed. Ask for the grace of forgiveness and feel the release that goes with accepting that as fully as possible. This may involve you in a conversation directed to that higher power.

    It may be you use prayers you are familiar with, even if it has been some time since they were used last! The important thing is the sincerity of your intent, the focus of your concentration, and that you open to the feelings that go with the exercise.

4. Now imagine that the Divine image that you have invoked is so moved by your sincere entreaty that it responds directly. If you are relating to a figure, you will see them smile warmly, and sense their love and compassion welling up. Then see that energy growing in the form of light within their heart. If using the more abstract image of the sun like a ball of light, feel the response and see the light growing within the ball of light. Next imagine a stream of this radiant light flowing down towards you — a stream of pure white radiant light — a stream of loving kindness. As this light reaches you, you either breathe it in for the first exercise, or feel it flow through you as it does in the next.

Either way you continue to feel the light flow into your body until every part is immersed in light. This light has the quality and nature to purify you on every level. It transforms illness and generates radiant physical vitality. It releases negative emotions and thoughts, purifying and cleansing you on every level.

5.   As this sense of healing, cleansing and vitality builds, the light glows stronger. Feel now as if your body itself dissolves into the light.

6.   Next it is as if this body of light rises up to merge into the Divine Source and becomes one with it.

7.   Rest in this blissful state of oneness as long as possible.

8.   Complete the exercise consciously. When you feel it time to stop, take a few minutes to bring your awareness back to your body. It usually helps to move your feet a little, perhaps feel your hands move a little and then have a gentle stretch.

There are special needs for those people who do not have a good sense of their own personal boundaries or who know they have given a lot of their own power away and are trying to reclaim it. Before you finish, re-establish a sense of your own boundaries, your own personal space. What is needed is often more than the basic feeling of being back in your body. To explain — if you approach another person, there comes a point where you feel too close, as if you are entering into their space and it gets uncomfortable (especially presuming you do not know them too well). Where that point is will be at the edges of your personal space. So some people find it worthwhile to re-establish this boundary consciously before they complete this exercise. You can do this as a separate Imagery exercise, some people actually move their hands around their body to reinforce it.

Sometimes too, it can be both useful and pleasant to make time merely to sit quietly after this exercise, especially if it has been powerful and really touched you.

9.   As you move off to engage the rest of your day, aim to take the qualities that you experienced in the exercise with you. Carry the feelings of loving kindness in your heart and aim to be conscious of them throughout the day.

White Light Imagery — The Practice

When practising the White Light Imagery exercise, always follow the standard preliminaries recommended for Imagery. Make sure you take time to consciously relax physically and calm your mind using the principles of the Relaxation Response.

When it comes to the actual practice you may be able to read from the book, absorb the technique and then follow it through for yourself. However, this is certainly a technique which is helped in the learning by being with a teacher or using a tape. You could record the exercises yourself and play them back to assist your concentration. I have a tape and CD available featuring both of the exercises.

The White Light Imagery Exercise Using Breath

The White Light Imagery featuring the use of the breath was first recorded on pages 185–189 of *Peace of Mind*. It is reproduced here in smaller print so as to make it easier to refer to. This same exercise is on Side B of my Tape No. 4 — Guided Imagery Exercises.

> *This is a powerful imagery sequence which you will find rejuvenates and revitalizes you and it is a wonderful way to catalyse self-healing and convey your love and healing wishes to others.*

> *Once you are comfortably seated, let your eyes close gently ... turn your thoughts inwards ... remember that this is a time for healing ...*

> *Feel your body relaxing ... feel the muscles becoming soft and loose ... feel your weight begin to settle down*

into your chair, your muscles relaxed ... feel any tension releasing ... feel yourself relaxing deeply ... completely ... more and more ... deeper and deeper ... letting go ... feel it all through the body ... feel it deeply ... completely ... it is a good feeling ... a natural feeling ... feel the letting go ... feel it in the forehead particularly ... feel the forehead smoothing out ... feel it all through ... more and more ... deeper and deeper ... letting go ... completely ... deeply ... letting go ... more and more ... deeper and deeper ... letting go ... letting go ... letting go ...

Now become aware of your breathing ... it is not important whether it be fast or slow — just become aware of your breathing, whether it is fast or slow ... the breath moving in and out ... and, as you do, imagine that you are breathing in a pure white vapour ... so, with each breath in, see this pure white light moving down through your nostrils, down into your chest and filling it with a pure white light ... and, as you breathe out, imagine that you are releasing a grey light, a grey vapour, that carries with it all the old, the worn, and the unwanted ... as you breathe in again, imagine that you are breathing in the pure white light and bringing with it all that is pure, and fresh, and vital ... breathing out and releasing the old, and the worn, and anything unwanted in your system ... breathe it out and release it.

Now, while this is happening, you may choose to imagine that the white light is originating from your idea of the Divine ... it emanates from the Divine ... and, if you conceive the Divine to have a form, then see it in that shape and imagine the white light spreading from its heart ... so, if it be an elderly, male figure, see this bright light spreading from that figure's heart ... if it be from someone like Mother Mary, see the white light spreading forth from her heart ... if it be some other form, see the white light spreading down towards you ... and if, for you, the Divine is more abstract, perhaps it may suit you to see the focus, the centre of this light, as being like the sun and imagining the white light as streaming forth from the sun as representing the centre of the Divine, radiating out a pure white light in your direction ... and so imagine that from that source the white light streams forth and, as you breathe in, it passes down through your nostrils, down into your chest, filling it with all that is pure, clean, vital, healthy, and whole ... and as you breathe out, release the grey, the old, the worn, and the unwanted ... so that, with each new breath in, you bring, from the Divine, a pure white light that fills your chest and, as you breathe out, you release any old and worn energy ... anything at all you want to be free of ... and allow yourself to settle into a rhythm ... breathing in the pure white light, seeing it streaming down into your chest, and breathing out the grey ... in with the white and pure ... out with the grey, the old, and the worn ...

And, as you continue, feel the white light coming down steadily into your chest, and the strength of the light in your chest, growing stronger, and brighter, and purer, displacing any old and worn and grey areas, filling your whole chest with a pure white light ... a symbol of wholeness, purity, vitality, and healing ... you may be feeling the white light too, as a warmth, like a gentle warm liquid spreading through you ... perhaps it even tingles a little as it goes ...

With each new breath, draw in more white light, till your chest feels like it is aglow, filled with this pure white light, so that it feels it is radiating pure white light ... and, as you breathe in again, you feel the white light beginning to spill over, travelling down into your tummy ... as you breathe out now, you can direct the white light, down into your tummy and, as you see the white light travelling down, feel it relaxing ... feel it releasing ... feel it healing ... purifying ... and feel the warm white light travelling down, relaxing, releasing ... feel the warmth, the relaxation, the softness ... releasing any old and worn energy ... releasing any areas that are uncomfortable, painful ... feel them being filled with the white light, with its comfort, releasing ... and, as you breathe in now, draw in more pure white light from its source ... see it travelling down into your chest ... and, as you breathe out, radiate that white light down ... down through your abdomen ... down into your pelvis ... releasing any tension ... softening ... bringing warmth ... relaxation ... deeply ... breathing in more white light and seeing it travelling down now into your legs ... down your thighs ... softening ... releasing ... filling with a new strength ... purity ... bringing healing ... and wholeness ...

Breathing in more white light ... seeing it passing down now, down into your calves ... down into your feet ... releasing any tension ... releasing any old and worn areas ... and bringing a new vitality ... bringing healing ... strength ... so that now your legs, too, are filled with this pure, bright white light ...

And, as you breathe in again, direct the white light now down your arms and feel the relaxation, the release ... the softening, as your muscles loosen still more ... right down ... feel the light travelling right down into your fingers ... feel them soft and loose ... see them filled with the pure white light ... symbol of purity ... a feeling of natural vitality ...

As you breathe in again, draw more of the pure white light from its source ... see it filling your lungs ... and now see it travelling up your neck ... into your head ... and, as it moves upwards, feel the muscles relaxing ... feel them becoming soft and loose ... feel any old areas being released ... any worn areas ... let-

ting go ... any diseased areas being freed, and replaced with a pure white light ... symbol of new strength ... of purity ... of purity ... of healing ... of whole vitality ...

So, now feel your whole body filled with this pure white light and, with each new breath in, draw more white light from its source ... and see it filling your body with still more white light, so that your whole body is glowing intensely with the pure white light ...

And, as you breathe in more, see the white light expanding out, beyond your body ... to encapsulate you, like an egg ... like a cocoon of bright, pure, white light ... filling you with strength and vitality ... feel it as whole ... feel its unity ... feel yourself to be at one with it ... allow yourself to merge in the purity of the white light ... feel its Divine Source moving through you ... feel yourself to be at one with it ... feel yourself at peace ... be still ... feel it all through ... deeply ... completely ... all through ... feel yourself at one ... and be still ...

As you feel its sense of wholeness through you, you may now like to direct that white light to someone you care for ... to share that feeling with them ... and so imagine them where you can, doing whatever ... and imagine that, as you breathe in, the white light passes through you and radiates like a searchlight to the person you care for ... and see them filled with its whiteness ... see their body glowing white ... and see them surrounded in a cocoon of pure white light ... a symbol for purity ... for wholeness ... for healing ... for renewed vitality ...

And, as you breathe in, draw in more white light and radiate it to this person ... seeing them filled with a new wholeness ... a new sense of balance ... purpose ... seeing them whole and healthy ... pure and vital

... and share your experience with them ... feel them, too, filled with the pure white light ... and add your blessing ...

Allow yourself to merge again with the feeling of purity and wholeness of the light ... breathe in ... breathe in more white light ... see it streaming down from the Divine ... pouring into you like a funnel ... a funnel coming down through your nose and filling your body, and then radiating out ... spreading out around you ... and spreading off through your house ... around wherever you are ... see it filling with the pure white light ... and then it radiating further ... filling your house ... everyone in it ... filling them with purity, wholeness, health, and vitality ... feel your love flowing with it ... feeling that warm, happy feeling going with it ...

As you breathe in more, draw down more of this energy ... as you breathe out, radiate it beyond the house ... to the people around you ... to the houses around you ... feel it moving off, across the country ...

Breathing in more white light ... drawing it down, like a funnel ... drawing it down from the Divine ... through your body, and out across the land ... spreading out, so that you can imagine the whole country bathed in this pure white light ...

Breathing in more white light ... breathing it out, and feeling it travelling right around the globe ... wrapping the whole planet in a pure white light ... and share your feeling of peace and unity with the whole planet ... radiate that feeling out, and feel it travelling right around, so that the whole planet is held like a ball of pure white light ...

As you breathe in more, feel that white light streaming down ... feel yourself again merging with it ... feel it entering every part of your being ... feel your-

self at one with its purity ... at one with its peace ... one with its healing ... feel yourself at one with its vitality ... and realize that that white light symbolises Love in action ... allow yourself to merge into that feeling of Love, that Divine Love, streaming down and filling your whole being ... feel it all through ... feel its peace ... be still ... feel yourself merging with the stillness, to allow it to be all through you ... completely ... completely ... be still ...

The White Light Imagery Exercise Using Radiant Energy

This exercise was first recorded in *Meditation — Pure & Simple* (pages 102–104) and is reproduced here. This exercise is also on my CD *Relaxation, Meditation & Imagery*.

Take up your position, relax physically.

Imagine now, as if it were in the sky above you, the highest source of power that you know. The embodiment of your own Truth. It may be an image that symbolizes God, it may be the figure of Christ, Mother Mary or a particular saint. You may prefer a more abstract image such as the sun which could represent the source of Universal Energy. Whichever of these symbolic images you find most helpful, imagine too that as well as a source of energy, this is a source of love and compassion, of loving kindness, of a presence that has your own best interest at heart.

As this image forms in your mind, allow yourself to imagine what it would feel like to come into the presence of this Divine Source of Energy. What would it be like to feel yourself in the presence of God? Or Christ? Or the source of Universal Energy?

Sometimes as you feel yourself coming closer to that presence, you may wish to say something — a prayer, an explanation, a request. Sometimes, something may be said to or for you, so you could listen for that.

Once you feel this Divine presence as if it is in the sky above you, imagine that a beam of white light begins to flow from its very centre, down towards you. An outpouring of energy and loving kindness. If you are focussed upon a figure, imagine this light flowing from its very heart. If you are using the sun, imagine the shaft of light flowing from its very centre.

Imagine too, that this beam of white light has liquid properties. It is like a beam of liquid white light that has a pleasant warmth to it, almost like a gentle glow.

Now as this beam of warm, liquid, white light reaches your head, it not only flows down around your body, but also it flows through your body. Warm, liquid, white light, slowly flowing down through your body. Almost like water filtering down through dry sand.

Warm liquid white light, flowing from that Divine source and flowing down through every part of your body. Like having a wash on the inside. It washes away anything old or worn or unwanted. It brings with it a new energy, a vitality, a sense of healing and wholeness. You can feel it filling your body and your being. You may see this quite visually or you may have it as a feeling experience — like feeling a flow of energy or a sensation of warmth moving down through your body. When the light does flow down to the end of your arms it will flow out the end of the fingers. When it does reach the end of your legs, it will flow out through the feet, washing away with it anything old, worn or unwanted.

When this light comes to difficult, tense, painful or blocked areas, it washes through them, clearing them, relaxing them, letting them go. You may see the affected area as having a particular shape and/or colour. When the light reaches such an area, you may see that colour being washed away like a stain washed away from clothes held under running water. You may see the area dissolved from the outside in. Some people find it helpful to imagine the light being concentrated almost like a laser. This then burns away the affected blockage — either from the outside in or from the inside out.

The aim is to see and feel this warm liquid light to be filling every part of the body with the same degree of intensity. To feel the same all over. Filled with the vigour, the vitality, the radiance of the warm liquid white light.

As this feeling becomes all-encompassing, it is as if you merge with it; almost as if you dissolve into the light. You feel it through your body and your mind. It is as if you become at one with it. Given that it stems from a Divine source, this can feel like merging or re-uniting with the Divine. It can be a powerful experience.

You conclude by merely resting in the presence of that light and the Divine Energy it represents and carries.

These are both key exercises. If you were only to do one form of Imagery practice, this would be the one to start with. The more you do it, and the more you enter into the spirit of the exercises, the more it will bring your spirituality to life.

While these exercises start by consciously invoking a spiritual presence, many people find that this spiritual energy does come to life, that it does take on a reality that can be experienced directly. With this direct experience comes a knowing, a certainty, a sense of connectedness that is deeply satisfying. These are the experiences that transform your life as they confirm all the finest things you may have hoped for.

MANIFESTATION

Discussion of the principles and practice of Manifestation are included in this Chapter as this too is a key spiritual practice.

The purification of motive and past actions that is possible with the White Light Imagery exercise, and the balanced view that comes with it, coupled with the simple stillness of meditation, are all excellent and necessary preludes for sound Manifestation.

Manifestation is based on the simple spiritual view that your needs will be met. It takes the great spiritual teachings literally. For example the classical Christian text is:

> '*Ask and it will be given to you; seek, and you will find; knock, and it will be opened to you. For everyone who asks receives, and he who seeks finds, and to him who knocks it will be opened.*'　　　　　(Luke 11, 9–10)

This theme of needs being met is expanded upon with images of the birds and the lilies in the field being fed and clothed (Luke 12, 13–48).

In the way that we are discussing it here, Manifestation is to do with the big issues such as finding the right partner, house, therapist, job etc. It does have equal application to lesser things like meeting day to day needs such as manifesting car parking spaces! Often in fact the lesser issuescan act like a training ground to experiment with the technique, to see results, gain confidence and move on to the larger issues.

When it comes to the big issues, the key elements for Manifestation are the clarity and purity of intention, backed by a deep trust in genuine needs being met. For example towards the end of my illness, Grace and I travelled to India to visit Sai Baba. At this pivotal moment, he told me that I was already healed and not to worry. This confronted me with the choice of going on as I had been, half hoping to get well, or making the leap to Faith and going on with conviction. Making that leap, I also made a silent vow to myself that when I recovered I would make a return visit in gratitude.

A year later I was well, Grace was pregnant with our first child, we were living in Queensland and broke! I arranged to lease a Veterinary practice in Adelaide and we decided that while on the move we would go via India! With virtually no money in our account we booked the tickets, sent a cheque, and hoped that in some wonderful way it would be honoured.

The tickets arrived, we went, had an amazing series of adventures in India and returned. Years later we still wondered where the money came from! It turned out that about a year before all this had taken place I had asked my parents to raise some money for me by selling a very special painting I had bought in better times. This had taken some time and, amidst all else, it had slipped our minds. When the painting sold, my parents put the money into my account, but, as it happened, we had just left for India and they actually forgot to tell us on our return. Between us all we did not realize the synchronicity until years later!

Some may call it coincidence. I am happy with synchronicity, but in truth it may be better described as Manifestation! During my illness, these principles were so dramatically and so repeatedly demonstrated for Grace and myself, that the reality of all this for me is beyond doubt. After I was well, we returned to the Philippines and I was taught the essence of Manifestation as it applies to healing and life itself by a great traditional Filipino healer. Mr Terte spoke to me with a passionate fervour, teaching me these techniques literally on the night before he died.

Mr Terte also went to some lengths to caution me, as I would caution anyone contemplating using these techniques. While the principles and techniques are relatively simple and work profoundly, your motivation can markedly affect any personal cost they may have. This is where ego is the big trap.

If you want something from a place of greed, desire, even aversion; if your ego is the driving motivational force behind Manifestation and if, as you may well do, you succeed in Manifesting what you want in this way, it will rebound upon you. In the simplest terms this means whatever you gain from this ego-driven place will back-fire on you. You will lose it, it will turn sour, it will come back to haunt you. I am hoping that this is clear enough to be a little scary and that it makes an impression. Do take this seriously. The key step in Manifestation is to separate your wants from your needs. When there is a genuine, heartfelt need that has a pure motive, then Manifestation is how you bring it into being in a conscious, joyful and effective way. When the motive is pure all that happens is that you need to give thanks for what comes. Then you are free to celebrate the process as well as whatever was manifested.

The Principles of Manifestation

Mr Terte was in his late seventies when he died. He had been responsible for reviving the traditional healing technique of Psychic Surgery in the Philippines and had taught many, if not most of the younger healers. He had an extraordinary spiritual understanding and a huge presence. Mr Terte played a significant role in my own healing when Grace and I first visited him in 1976.

At the time we revisited the Philippines in 1979, Mr Terte developed gangrene, first in one leg, then the other. Grace and I helped to pay the medical bills for this grand old man; his life having been true to his principles, he had given all his money away. Initially he was hospitalized and we were asked to pay for the amputation of the gangrenous leg. It seemed an extraordinary situation! However, before the surgery could be performed, gangrene became established in his other leg and Mr Terte was taken to his daughter's home to die.

That evening in the half light of candles, Mr Terte, propped up on pillows and resting his head on one arm, spoke of all this. Mr Terte's English was only fair and for things like this he wanted to be clear. So he strung together quotes from the Bible, impatiently asking his family to read out the quotes. He gave the references, they were to read the passages. Humour came into it as Mr Terte grew frustrated with the time it took his daughter to find the passages. He would grab the Bible, and knowing it so thoroughly, open it at the right page and thrust it back to be read.

In essence, what Mr Terte said is that both healing and manifestation are carried out through the action of Faith, Prayer and the Holy Ghost. What did he mean by that?

Faith is faith in a spiritual framework that has a sense of abundance, of needs being met, benevolence and trust.

Prayer is the technique of clarifying needs and being able to ask confidently that they will be met.

The Holy Ghost is the Spirit in action. It is what provides the substance to the thought that makes it manifest in the physical world.

In more practical terms, we can identify the following steps in the process of Manifestation.

1. Establish a clear need.
    Differentiate between needs and wants. It has to be essential, pure, necessary. It can work if the motive is selfless service or giving to meet another's need. Far from ego-driven, it needs to be of the heart or spirit.

2. Have a solid framework of understanding.
    Here understanding is vital, just as it is in all Imagery work. To my mind what is needed here is an understanding of, and relationship with God. You may call it Universal Energy or Life Force or whatever. I like 'God.' Based on this knowing, this experience you have, this relationship, then there can be the confidence to ask and expect that your needs will be met.
    There may be some pre-requisites. You will probably be able to reflect a little and come up with your own list.

Consider forgiveness, reconciliation, spiritual commitment and practice, self worth, prayer, gratitude, an attitude that recognizes and honours the sacred in life. The sense that you have learnt from the past and it is time for change and new developments.

3. The ask.
   It may well be useful to pre-empt this with prayer — whether it be formal or of your own wording. I like the spirit behind:

   'Not as I would O Lord, But as thy will.'

   There is the accompanying sense of being a small fish in a little pond who can see a small part of a big picture (pardon the well worn images but they are useful ones!) This exercise is based in humility with the sense of doing the best you can, putting in your request and then trusting the outcome.

4. Let it go!
   This is a key step that is often tricky. Let it go. It is as if you make the ask, put it out to God or the Universe, and await the response. So you do not dwell on it. You do not worry or question. You wait in trust. Importantly, you do not let it go into some void or vacuum. You entrust your request to the higher power and wait in expectant anticipation.

5. Act where necessary.
   It may be enough to physically do nothing while you wait. There may be a lot to do. The important thing is to be clear enough within yourself to act true to yourself. Quite commonly this approach is an invitation to hard work! It is as if when you do all that you can within your own sphere, then the spiritual world with all its abundance is available to you and adds to your efforts. Be congruent, be authentic.

6. Avoid surprise.
   When what you ask for turns up, do all that you can to avoid being surprised! After all you were expecting your

needs to be met!

7.   Give thanks and celebrate.
This too is a vital step. Consciously address the power you made the request to. Give thanks. Delight in what happens. Guard against boasting or pride. Practise humility. Celebrate with a sense of joy.

8.   Develop trust.
With experience, this will come naturally. Not infrequently, however, needs can be met in ways that at the time seem puzzling. Often it seems that it takes the benefit of hindsight to be able to reflect back and make sense of *why* particular things happened when they did. An obvious and dramatic example of this is the many people who came to realize major illness was almost like a gift, as it turned their lives around for the better.

Trusting this principle of needs being met, deeply trusting, is both a challenge and a freedom.

9.   Accept responsibility.
In the Bible is the rejoinder:

'Every one to whom much is given, of him much will be required; and of him to whom men commit much they will demand the more.'   (Luke 12, 48)

Be humble, be modest, dedicate Manifestation to the higher good and the good of others.

My favourite way to begin teaching the use of these principles is with car parking spaces. I find it incredibly reliable as long as I ask at least five minutes before I get to the destination, as long as I am not surprised to find yet another park right outside where I want to go, and as long as I give thanks. Give it a try, practise in other areas. Manifestation is well worth applying consciously in the more important areas of your life.

CHAPTER 12

HEALING THE BODY — I

The Principles of Mind/Body Medicine

Sandy was in her late thirties, had two young children and a husband who was very successful in business. Her diagnosis of breast cancer devastated the family. Particularly as the cancer had already spread into her bones. After breast surgery, her ovaries were removed in the hope that it might slow down the progress of the disease.

When Sandy came to our cancer support group, she changed her diet, learnt to meditate and began to use Imagery. Sandy had difficulty seeing pictures to use in Imagery; she was strongly kinesthetic — she *felt* her images. She also had a strong Christian faith. So Sandy imagined the presence of God, as if He was in the sky above her, prayed and then felt a stream of healing energy flowing down through her head and into her body.

Sandy had seen her bone scan. She had two secondary cancers in her bones — one in the hip, the other in her ribs. When she saw the scan, her attention had focussed on the lesion in her hip; she had not really taken in the one in her ribs.

About eight weeks after diagnosis, Sandy and her family were required to make a major move to follow her husband's work. Sandy was keen to find out how her cancer was progressing, as this information may have affected their choices. Her doctors felt that at best her condition may be the same, they strongly implied it was likely to be worse. They were quite unprepared for what they found! The lesion in the ribs had remained unchanged — no worse, no better. Yet the lesion in the hip was not only better, the cancer was gone and the bone had regenerated completely. It was fully healed!

Sandy was delighted to share her good news with the group. She realized that she had formed a clear mental picture of the hip lesion, based upon what she had seen of her scan. With the Imagery, she was able to feel this flow of energy, coming from its Divine Source, and as it came into her body, she felt a flow of warmth come with it. She said that for her, she knew that the healing was flowing whenever she felt the warmth. Sandy realized, however, that while she had done this clearly and powerfully for the hip, she had neglected the ribs almost completely.

Obviously the next step was for Sandy to direct the healing energy to her ribs. She rang me a few days later very concerned. In attempting to do just that, she found strong feelings rising up that now she was neglecting the hip and that the cancer there would recur.

I asked Sandy how big her God was! She said her God was infinite. So I asked her to consider that she was drawing healing energy from this infinite source and then feeling that there was not enough to go around! She laughed at the limitation she was imposing, although it still took her about two weeks of practice before she felt fully comfortable with the notion of healing the second lesion while she adequately covered the rest of her body.

The move for Sandy and her family involved the usual pressures of major change, readjustment, renewing old relationships and making new beginnings. Shortly afterwards, and conscious of the potential affects of stress, Sandy had more tests. No change — the hip all clear, the ribs still affected. Three months later, a well settled Sandy had her next tests. All clear — healed hip, healed ribs — a remarkable recovery.

Sandy's story is a dramatic example of many cases where the use of specific forms of Imagery has brought specific results. Coincidence? There seems to be a lot more to it!

Sarah had a similar background and problem to Sandy. Except that Sarah had eleven bony secondaries that were diagnosed three years after her treatment for primary breast cancer. Sarah had seen her bone scans, fixed that image in her mind, was very visual in her Imagery and imagined each lesion healing. She received excellent support from her family and her local GP who was actually involved in Mind/Body medicine. Three months later, all the cancer was gone — except for one lesion in her hip. Sarah and her GP were puzzled by this until they checked with the original scan. Sarah had missed seeing the lesion in her hip! She had retained a clear picture of all the other spots, but missed this one. Three months later, at her next scan, the hip was clear too.

Steven's diagnosis of lung cancer led to major chest surgery with removal of the lower section of one lung. At the point where the wind pipe (bronchus) was severed to remove the lung, staples were used to seal it shut. Not long after the surgery, these staples popped open creating a broncho-pleural fistula — a large cavity filled with air in the chest. A CAT scan demonstrated that a large triangular area was affected.

Steven sought several opinions, hoping the lung might heal itself or that further surgery would fix it. His doctors were convinced that the breakdown had resulted from the activity of cancer that had been left after the surgery. They told Steven that the area remaining was like a buttery mass in his chest, that it could not heal itself and that further surgery was dangerous and unwarranted. They offered to wait and see, and that if it did improve perhaps they could staple it again. Steven pressed the doctors, asking if they were sure that it could not heal on its own. 'Absolutely; there is no way!' they stated emphatically.

Now Steven had some previous experience of meditation with Dr Ainslie Meares. This had helped him through a period of stress some twenty years earlier. Although he had let the practice slip, there was an experience, a foundation to build upon. And a sense of the possible. After coming to our residential program, Steven returned to intensive meditation and began a new practice — Imagery. Every day, he began his meditation sessions with ten to fifteen minutes of Imagery. He found that for him, the Imagery also made an ideal lead-in to the stillness of Meditation.

For his Imagery, Steven brought the CAT scan to mind. In a very visual way, he saw the lesion fairly literally. Then on a microscopic level, Steven imagined filling in the hole, using bricks of a wobbly, rectangular shape that for him represented new lung cells. In his mind he envisaged these bricks slowly building up, one on top of the other, reforming healthy lung tissue and closing the gap. Three months later, a rather incredulous doctor showed Steven a healthy CAT scan with the report 'The Broncho Pleural Fistula has spontaneously healed!' Spontaneously?! Steven is in no doubt that the meditation and the specific Imagery work was what did it.

So, how can we explain these cases, these anecdotes? Are they just coincidences? Is it just mind over matter — or is there more to it? I believe that there is a simple theoretical basis behind these remarkable true stories. This theory is based upon good science and when converted into practice through the use of Imagery, there is the potential to help many people overcome a wide range of illnesses.

To put Healing Imagery in its full context we need to go back to basics. The body has an extraordinary ability to heal itself. It is well designed to cope with both traumas and diseases. The body's basic urge is to maintain itself in that dynamic state of balance we call health.

No doubt we have all had times where we drank too much or ate too much, and perhaps quite literally we were knocked off balance. However, the body is like a spinning top — when it is knocked off balance, its natural tendency is to virtually automatically return to that state of balance. And it does it so well!

We know that if we cut a finger, the body's natural reaction is to initiate a complex array of healing mechanisms that seal the cut, regenerate new tissues and restore normal function. With a broken bone, the healing mechanisms are even more complex and wonder-full — that is they are full of wonder in their intricacy and their capacity to heal. No doubt too, we have all experienced some sort of infection in our lives — colds, flu, abscesses, gastric disease. Again, the body has an amazing ability to meet these challenges, overcome them and to restore the balance we equate with good health.

Now, to understand this a little more, we need to appreciate how these healing mechanisms are controlled. In the late sixties and early seventies when I went through my Veterinary training, not much was known of all this. We did know, for example, that the immune system plays a major role in the body's defences. Also we knew that there was cellular immunity too — that the cells of the body themselves had some capacity to resist infection and even cancer.

However, these healing mechanisms were thought to operate largely independently, and in a way removed from any central nervous system or mind control.

Current knowledge has come a long way. It is now well known that the brain directly affects healing in two major ways. The first is by the wide variety of chemicals it produces, the other is via direct nerve pathways.

What we now know is that different states of mind, different feelings, different emotions, produce different and quite specific chemicals in the brain. These chemicals, called neurotransmitters, neuropeptides or more simply, messenger molecules — are then released into the blood stream. Travelling in the blood they then flow to cells of the immune system. Here they attach onto specific receptor sites on the outer membranes of those cells. This in turn triggers changes within the cells that can dramatically affect their function.

This then, is another key point. It is not only a matter of how many immune cells you have, it is a matter of how actively and effectively they are functioning. For a long time it has been known that white blood cells are the front line for the immune system. For a long time it has been known that having too many of these cells is a problem, just as it is to have too few.

More recent research, however, has revealed that you could have the right number, but that they could still range in function from inactive and so ineffective, to highly active and highly effective. Clearly then to have an active immune system is a strong prerequisite for both good health and active healing.

The key to Mind/Body medicine is that negative thoughts readily depress immune function, positive thoughts activate it. What this means is that if you are depressed, suffer unresolved grief, bottle your emotions, you are highly likely to release specific chemicals from your brain that will directly suppress immune function.

Happily, on the other hand, when you are inspired, feel a surge of hope or love, when you have a good laugh, other different and again, quite specific messenger molecules are released from the brain, travel via the bloodstream, attach to immune cells and activate them markedly.

Furthermore, quite remarkably, it is now known that cells of the immune system, the white blood cells, produce their own messenger molecules that they too release into the blood stream. These molecules return to the brain giving feedback and completing the loop of communication between the mind and the healing functions of the body.

What this means in effect is that there is a healing centre in the brain that has a great capacity to control and regulate healing throughout the body. This is very similar to the fact that we have a running centre in the brain. By this I mean that when you decide to go for a run, the idea starts as a conscious thought in your mind. However, when it comes to the actual act of the running, that is a very complex process. Fortunately you do not need to think how to move this leg and that, how to combine those movements in a rhythm with your arms, how to regulate your heart rate and your breathing. All that is controlled by the automatic part of the brain. The process of going for a run then is that first there is the conscious thought 'I will go for a run.' Then that conscious thought goes down into the unconscious, automatic part of the brain which picks up the message, recognizes it and says 'Sure, I know how to do that; how fast do you want to go?' Again, using conscious intention, we may give the message to speed up or slow down, while the actual process of running is under this automatic direction.

Now, everyone it seems has needed to go to the trouble of learning how to connect the conscious desire to run, with the automatic centre that actually does it for us. I love watching young children learning to walk and run. You see them struggle up onto their feet, usually hanging onto a chair or table leg. And you can see the thought form 'I'm going to walk across the room.' And off they go, full of hope, full of expectation. A few tottery steps and crash! Down they go. Now I am yet to see a toddler just lie there, give up and say 'Well, I guess I'm going to be one of those kids who never learns to walk!' No, it seems so natural. They get up, try again, and again, and finally they master it.

So it seems that most of us have taken the time to learn how to connect the conscious mind with the brain's running centre. What I suggest is that the same potential is there to control the healing centre, it is just that most of us have not yet learnt how to connect with it.

What we need then, is a reliable mechanism that would connect the conscious intention 'I want to heal,' with that automatic, unconscious part of the brain that regulates that healing. We need a link between the conscious mind and the unconscious. Sound familiar?! Obviously what provides this link is the creative use of Imagery.

In healing, as elsewhere, Imagery provides a link between the conscious intention and the automatic function.

We can use Imagery as a vehicle to carry a specific message (concerning a need to heal in a specific way) from the conscious mind, through the healing centre and on directly to the body's wonderful array of healing mechanisms.

Before we move into the techniques that make all this possible, another important reminder of the value of meditation and balance. Do remember that in the simple silence of meditation we return to a profound sense of balance and that in that state, healing is free to flow naturally.

So the question often arises, 'In healing is meditation enough or should I do Imagery only? Or a bit of both?'

I encourage everyone who is engaged actively in healing to practise simple, passive meditation. It provides that deep sense of balance, a stable foundation from which to work and within which to heal.

About three-quarters of the people affected by cancer that I help, take up the practice of Imagery. It is particularly helpful for people when recently diagnosed, particularly if they have their own fears and anxieties for the future or have been *pointed* by being given bad news badly and having their hope taken away. Imagery is usually easy for people who have active minds, who can concentrate well and who are used to working with their minds. It combines particularly well with any form of treatment, providing a direct means to support that treatment with the active and creative power of the mind.

The principles to have strongly in mind with the use of Healing Imagery, are that, as for other Imagery exercises, the images be accurate, complete and feel good to use. This latter point is of particular importance. Often when you begin Imagery, you know that it could be better, you have the sense that as a beginner you are learning, but it feels good. You feel confident with where you are with it, against the background of knowing that with time and more practice the actual technique will improve. This sense of feeling confident with your Imagery is a vital ingredient in its successful application.

Remember too, that when it comes to technique, we can use three types of Imagery — Literal, Symbolic or Abstract. Obvious healing is another area where the actual doing of it is a complex interaction of many processes that really are far better suited to being controlled by that automatic, unconscious Healing Centre of the brain, than by direct conscious act of will. So Literal images have very limited use although as the examples we have already used demonstrate, semi-literal images (such as CAT scans, X-rays, and photographs of immune cells etc.) can provide a useful starting point for the Imagery.

Now to put it all into practice!

CHAPTER 13

HEALING THE BODY — II

How to use Imagery for healing

Almost invariably, Symbolic or Abstract Imagery will work best for healing. To begin with, here then is a summary of the necessary steps for the use of Symbolic Imagery.

How to use Symbolic Imagery for Healing — the Principles

1. Develop Symbolic Images that represent:
    a) the illness
    b) any treatment
    c) the immune system and other aspects of the body's healing mechanisms.

2. Combine these images into a sequence of action in a way that removes the image of the illness and replaces it with a symbol of fully restored health.

3. Check that these symbols are accurate and complete and that you can feel good using them.

4. Support your practice with Meditation, other Imagery exercises where necessary, and the general principles of Positive Thinking.

5. Assess your progress, modify or adapt your Imagery as required. You may well find that over the longer term the urge to practise Imagery declines and you feel more fully satisfied with the ongoing practice of Meditation.

Symbolic Imagery for Healing — the Practice

1.   Developing the Images

The most important thing when developing your own symbolic images is that they feel good for you. They need to provide an accurate image that represents the illness for you in a way that is acceptable intellectually, and even more importantly, intuitively. There seems to be four main ways that people derive these images:

(i)   By being inspired by other people's images

Sometimes as you read of other people's Imagery or listen to others discuss it, you are inspired and your own image springs to mind. Having said that, in my experience it rarely works if you try to take on someone else's images just because it worked for them. As we have discussed, Imagery, especially Symbolic Imagery, is very personal, so the best images are the ones that you come up with yourself and can identify with very directly.

A good example was an elderly lady who came to me having read the Simonton's excellent book *Getting Well Again* (a must to read if you are using Healing Imagery). Margaret had read of their recommendation to use aggressive images. She latched on to their suggestion to imagine the cancer as being like lumps of meat in the body, the immune system as being a pack of savage, hungry dogs that were let loose to race around the body and greedily gobble up the meat (alias the cancer). As Margaret described these dogs in detail, I recoiled at the terrifying picture she made of it. Asking her what she felt about these dogs, Margaret replied, 'Well, actually, they scare me to death!' When I asked her how she felt about being scared to death by an image that represented her own immune system, she realized she needed to change the picture!

Talking on, it became apparent that Margaret's passion in life was her garden. So, together we worked out that she could imagine her body to be a beautiful garden, the cancer would be a particular form of weed and that her immune system was a very wise and diligent old gardener. Margaret's chemotherapy would be a weed killer that had a very selective action. It would kill the (cancer) weeds very effectively, but the rest of the garden (her body) would be unaffected. In fact, the gardener would add compost to the garden, representing the good food that made up Margaret's new diet. With all this, the garden would thrive.

We now had an accurate image that Margaret could feel good about, but to me there was a sense that it still could be incomplete. Being a gardener myself, my experience is that once a new weed comes into the garden, you get rid of it, but often it comes back. Questioning Margaret on this, I found that her experience matched mine. So, to off-set the subtle implication in the image, and the real possibility of natural recurrence, we added to the Imagery sequence. As well as spraying the weeds, Margaret's gardener was then sent on regular patrol, to seek out any new signs of weed growth and to eliminate them before they developed into any serious problem. He also was to constantly tend and support the garden, making it healthier and stronger — so healthy that illness had no part in it.

(ii) Through the use of semi-literal images

All the examples at the start of this Chapter, featured the use of semi-literal images based upon scans or X-rays. For Sandy, Sarah and Steven, what they had literally seen as a representation of their cancers (the scans and X-rays) formed the starting point for very effective Imagery.

It is hard to predict who will be best suited to which type of Imagery, but it is easy to imagine that more literal, left-brained people may be drawn to this type of semi-literal Imagery; whereas the more creative types prefer the symbols. While there have been plenty of exceptions to these rules, people with a medical background often find the semi-literal approach appealing.

Tom was a specialist surgeon who had a rather rare and particularly nasty cancer intertwined around his spine. He was well aware of his poor medical prognosis and treatment was regarded as being purely palliative. Tom had a very detailed anatomical knowledge of the area affected by the cancer. He studied his X-rays and scans to form a clear picture of the extent of the cancer and the damage it had done to his spine.

He then formed a very clear picture in his mind of what the area would look like when healed again. Tom proceeded to imagine the cancer shrivelling, and the healthy tissue regenerating. He had a remarkable response to his 'palliative' treatment, the cancer disappeared and normal function of his spine returned.

We have found that it often helps people to get a strong image of what healthy, healed tissue looks like. So often it can help people with liver disease to go to the butcher and actually ask to see a healthy liver. This image can then be held in mind as the end goal.

(iii)   Out of the stillness of Meditation

Very often, once people have learnt the background to Imagery, it works well to contemplate the principles, reflect on them deeply, and then wait for the images to arise spontaneously. This is a reliable process that has worked well for many people.

Henri had prostate cancer with multiple bony secondaries. He found great comfort in using the Quiet Place Imagery as a lead-in to meditation. His place was sitting on a large flat rock, beside a river that was near his childhood home. As he learnt about Healing Imagery, a spontaneous image came to mind. Henri imagined sitting on his rock and taking one of the affected bones out of his arm. In his mind he had no trouble imagining washing it in the river! He even kept a large bottle brush by the rock which he pushed up through the marrow of the bone, washing out all the cancer as he rinsed it in the river. He saw the cancer as a dark red stain that the river washed away, and he enjoyed seeing the colour trailing away downstream. Once the first bone was sparkling clear, he put it back and moved on to take out and clean the next. Henri went on to have a remarkable long-term recovery.

(iv)   Have the body produce the Image

Charles was an accountant who had led a highly stressed, if fairly successful business life. When bowel cancer was diagnosed with inoperable liver secondaries, Charles attended our residential programs more out of desperation than conviction. During meditation sessions, we often apply light touch in the way of Dr Ainslie Meares. This helps people to relax more directly and often helps focus their attention on particular areas. Sometimes it helps people to form an Image of their illness.

Charles had been having little success with his Meditation or Imagery. His busy mind seemed to be ever active, that is, until he felt the gentle hands in Meditation. At first he knew they belonged to one of our therapeutic team. He felt deeply reassured by the touch, deeply calmed. His thoughts settled, he could feel his state of mind changing. Then the hands left only to be replaced by two more hands. Two hands that had an even stronger quality. Charles, a long time agnostic, swears they were the hands of Christ! They filled him with a sense of unconditional love, they brought a heat and energy to his liver. He began to sweat, he began to smile. He was deeply moved. He felt that healing had begun.

The feeling of the hands stayed with Charles as a part of a powerful image. The whole experience transformed his attitude; he began on a healing path, he began the spiritual journey. Many years later, Charles has survived liver secondaries longer than anyone his experienced specialists know of.

For others, putting their own attention into the area of their cancer, or touching the area lightly themselves, is effective in drawing forth an image from the cancer itself.

Images derived in this way are invariably very relevant, very powerful and when used in this way, very effective.

2.   **Practising the sequence of Healing**

This is where all the principles of Imagery come into action. Most people are able to see their Imagery sequence as you might watch a video or cartoon sequence. Some talk their way through the healing sequence too, either just describing to themselves what is happening, or repeating affirmations as the pictures run. Wherever possible, it is ideal to add a physical sensation to the Imagery. For some this means having a sensation of a flow of energy, for others feelings of warmth attend the healing.

Ideally, it is best to imagine the healing sequence taking place in the location of the illness itself. This means that rather than imagining that the healing pictures are running (literally) through your head, or on an imaginary screen in front of you, aim to focus your attention where the lesions are and superimpose the images on that place. Many people find it helpful to put their hands on or over the affected areas, so that this sense of the Imagery taking place at that point is strengthened.

To reiterate, the aim of the healing sequence is to start with an image of the illness, for the treatment and immune system to combine to remove the illness and for the healthy tissue to regenerate. Steven's sequence was an excellent example of an image that powerfully symbolized the healthy tissue closing in and completing the healing.

3.   **Checking that the images are accurate, complete and feel good**

As stated frequently now, the risk with this practice is that the images may be inaccurate or incomplete, reflecting poor technique or deeper issues of doubt or self-sabotage. Very commonly the people I work with find that their first attempt at Healing Imagery produces useful images that remain at the core of their practice. However, it is very common that these initial images have limitations and that they can be improved upon.

The best way to check Healing Imagery is to draw your Imagery sequence. Ideally, you do this with someone who is experienced in the field, although a smart friend may well suffice. You explain your intention with the Imagery, what the symbols mean and how they interact. Against the need for accuracy and completeness, most outsiders will pick any deficiencies.

Nancy had stomach cancer with liver secondaries. The stomach had been cleared with surgery, but the liver remained a major problem. Nancy asked me to check her Imagery as she was committed to getting well and keen to pursue every possible avenue. She had seen a scan of her liver and had a clear picture of the extent of the three lesions in it. Nancy represented her immune system and other healing qualities with the symbol of 'Pacman.' Her pacman had two legs and big teeth! She knew she needed the right number of them; for her this meant that she needed a team of twelve! With this very personal Imagery, Nancy imagined that her twelve Pacmen lived in behind her liver. Three times a day she did her practice, bringing out the Pacmen (in her mind) and seeing them eat up the three cancer lesions before she put them back to rest behind her liver. The Imagery was accurate enough but clearly incomplete. Nancy was directing her healing to function fully three times a day for about five minutes each time (while she was actually doing the Imagery). For the rest of the day, she was instructing her immune system to rest! Clearly Nancy needed to have her healing operating twenty-four hours a day. This is how it normally operates anyway. However, faced with this suggestion, Nancy was deeply concerned that her Pacmen (the symbols for her immune system) would become tired and ineffective if they worked all day! What she could imagine, however, were two more teams of twelve. She set up a rotating roster, with each team having a shift while the other two rested! For Nancy this satisfactorily represented her immune system working fully and effectively. Nancy lived for many years, much longer than her doctors had ever thought possible.

4.   Supporting your Healing Imagery Practice

Imagery becomes a vehicle for positive expectations. It puts those hopes and beliefs into practice. Therefore your Imagery practice will be supported by anything that builds your confidence, develops your belief in the possibility of healing, and anything that generates Faith. There have been many helpful things covered in this book — the benefits of simple meditation and specific positive thinking exercises with the use of Affirmations and other forms of Imagery. Do recognize the value of an integrated approach and be reminded of the company you keep.

The attitudes, hopes and beliefs of those around you can influence your own situation strongly. We have witnessed this repeatedly with young children battling cancer. Jane had an eighteen month old child Nathan who was not responding to his cancer treatment. His doctors had told Jane and her husband Roger that they were sorry, nothing seemed to be working and they did not expect Nathan to live long. Jane changed Nathan's diet onto simple wholesome food and she and Roger learnt to meditate and how to practise Imagery. At least twice a day when Nathan was asleep, one or both of his parents would cradle him in their arms, enter their own state of Meditation and imagine what they felt was also encompassing Nathan. They imagined him wrapped in a warm blanket of loving, healing light that was all around, and all through him. As his treatment continued, they did specific Healing Imagery for him, imagining the Imagery projected onto his tiny body. Remarkably, his condition began to improve. To his doctor's amazement, Nathan went on to make a full recovery and is now a healthy teenager.

Partners can share Meditation and Imagery with the patient. This needs to be done as free of ego as possible

— as free of desire and longing as possible. It is a big ask to let go of the selfish motives, and to move into a space of unconditional loving kindness, but here is an important and necessary caution. If you attempt to do this type of exercise for someone you love or care for, and find you are doing it with a sense of desperation or urgency, you may be better to leave it. You need to have a perspective that understands that in doing this exercise you are not taking on exclusive responsibility for the outcome. In other words, this exercise can help but it is only one factor. Whether your partner gets well or not will depend on many issues. What is being said here is to do your best, but do not set yourself up for mental anguish or guilt. Do the best you can, that is all you can do.

Be aware too, that the beliefs or images held by other key people around you also could have an effect. Larry Dossey in his excellent book *Healing Words* discusses the power of prayer and the impact of thought on healing. It is quite conceivable that if your doctor has a strong belief as to your disease's outcome, then those thoughts will have some impact. For people with cancer it is essential that if you are aiming for recovery, that your key medical people can imagine you as a long-term survivor. I regularly suggest patients discuss this with their doctors and persist until they find a practitioner who can support them in this very important way.

5. **Assess your progress, adapt as necessary**

When you set yourself specific goals, it is important to assess your progress. With healing, assessments can range from easy to difficult, depending upon what types of tests may be needed for useful feedback. How often to seek this feedback therefore, will depend upon how quickly it seems the condition can change and how invasive any tests may be. I am a strong advocate of backing up your inner feelings and intuition with a reality check in the physical world. While mind, heart and spirit have a major and profound impact on our lives, it is still a physical body we live in, so I value physical assessments and reassessment.

Quite often Imagery does change with time and with healing progress. Ellie's story in Chapter One was a good example. Another concerned Tessa who had secondary spread of breast cancer into lymph nodes under her arm. She had a Pacman image (no legs, big teeth!) which represented her healing. Three times a day she reinforced the sequence of healing by imagining the Pacmen gobbling up her cancer. Then one day, as she prepared to begin the Imagery, the Pacmen went on strike! They literally refused to do anything and stayed motionless. Tessa was deeply concerned, so I recommended she go for a checkup immediately. All her cancer had disappeared. She was in remission and it appeared her Pacmen were not prepared to waste their time! They were quite happy, however, to be sent off on patrol, roaming Tessa's body to make sure no relapse could become established.

Another major issue with healing and the repeated practice of Imagery, is the question of whether or not the image needs to change with each session. For example Judy had breast cancer which had been treated by surgery and radiotherapy. Now she had secondaries in her liver and was using Imagery to assist her healing. She had an excellent healing sequence that finished with an image of her liver being clear of cancer, returned to full health. What bothered her deeply was that when she went to do her Imagery at the next session (she was doing it twice each day) there was the cancer again. Sure she could imagine getting rid of it again, but by going back to the beginning each time, was she recreating it? Should it get smaller each time or should it disappear altogether after just one effective Imagery exercise? Judy was confused.

This is a common problem for many people beginning healing Imagery. The practical answer to it is that you are using the Imagery to convey a conscious intention: 'I want to heal' directly to that automatic part of the brain, the Healing Centre, that controls the healing process. To achieve this goal, you are rehearsing the complete sequence of healing. What the Healing Imagery sequence represents therefore, is the complete process of healing, from what is known of the disease at the start, to the end point of complete health.

This is similar to the way we rehearse in our mind a physical journey from one place to another. We start at the beginning, imagine all the steps along the way and finish at the destination. In the case of healing, we are using the Healing Sequence to instruct the automatic Healing Centre in the brain what to do. We want it to take us from Disease to Health. We entrust the details of how to complete this (healing) journey to the Healing Centre. What we are aiming to do is to give it a very clear message of what we want — healing; so each time we do rehearse the whole sequence.

As feedback is not so easy with healing as when compared to a literal journey, usually we need to wait to gain that reassessment with tests taken from time to time. Then, based on that evidence we may modify or adapt the Imagery. Sometimes, as Nathan and Tessa's stories indicate, the Images will change spontaneously and predict or point to a change in the physical reality of the illness.

A final note on Symbolic Imagery in Healing. Many people have found Imagery to be a vital part of their healing journey. It seems fair to me to say that for many people it has played a pivotal role in catalysing remarkable healing. I have seen it happen often.

I always recommend that people who use active Imagery in this way, do reinforce it, do balance it with the practice of simple meditation. What I then notice is that very commonly, over time — perhaps six to twelve months — people come to feel that they have done enough Imagery; that the meditation seems complete in itself and that is what forms the basis of their ongoing daily practice. Often with time, people find that

Imagery is something they value, enjoy to use, but only do it from time to time when the need feels ripe. Often too, the Imagery they do persevere with tends to be of the more Abstract type. So let us conclude this section by considering Abstract Imagery.

Abstract Imagery for Healing

With Abstract Imagery we move from personally significant symbols to more abstract and Archetypal symbols. The two classical abstract healing images are light and water. Some exercises use one or the other, some use both light and water together. The two most common forms for using these images were detailed in Chapter Eleven on Invocation — the White Light Imagery Exercise using the breath (on pages 140–146) and the White Light Imagery exercise using an energy flow (pages 146–148)

It needs to be emphasized that these are excellent exercises for people who are healthy, as well as being powerful tools for healing. For well people, becoming familiar with White Light Imagery provides ready access to a major energy boost. When tired, you can do the exercise, draw on an infinite source of energy and rapidly revitalize your system. I have used this technique often on long car trips and found that it works very well for me.

For healing, the White Light Imagery exercises are the most common ones people use after coming to our programs. They are simple in their technique, combine the best of Imagery principles, are relatively free of complications, work well for many and always offer the added bonus of a very real, direct and profound spiritual experience.

When used for healing there are a few details to be aware of. An image for the illness is still required. Using a CAT scan image or X-ray for this often does link naturally with the image of water and/or light. Many people prefer to imagine the body in outline with the illness as a coloured lump. This technique is highly applicable for use with cancer and many other diseases. Once an image is formed for the disease, the light is drawn into the body with the breath, or flows in via the head, and then proceeds to remove the symbol of the illness.

White Light Healing Imagery using the Breath

Using the breathing based technique, you imagine the breath as a white vapour, seeing and feeling it (perhaps with a sensation of warmth or tingling) flowing towards the illness. Usually in this context the illness will feel harder and denser to you than the rest of the body. A common sensation is that it has some pain associated with it; it may also feel warmer than the rest of the body (occasionally some people feel it cooler.) Usually the illness will have a colour associated with it. As the white vapour of the breath reaches the illness, most commonly it swirls around the outside of the mass, dissolving it or perhaps causing it to burn or smoulder, releasing a grey vapour. This grey vapour, representing the residue of the illness, is then breathed out and released from the body.

White light (vapour) in with the breath, representing healing and all the life-affirming qualities coming in; grey light (vapour) out with the outbreath, representing the disease breaking down and being released, along with anything else, old, worn or unwanted that you need to release.

Many people find it helpful to breathe in the white vapour and to direct it into the centre of the illness, imagining the illness breaking down from the inside out, rather than from the outside in as above. It may help to focus the beam of light almost like a laser, and to imagine this concentrated shaft of light accentuating and accelerating the healing process.

White Light Healing Imagery using Energy Flow

Using the energy flow technique for White Light Imagery is similar in some respects except that now the light is imagined to have liquid properties as well. The liquid white light then flows down into the body and filters through it, quite slowly — a bit like water filtering down through dry sand. Again, this warm liquid white light gently but effectively washes away anything old, worn or unwanted! Often the disease can be imagined as a particular colour which can be seen to be washed away by the liquid light — a bit like a stain being rinsed from dirty clothes under a water tap. Also the liquid white light can be directly readily to particular areas that may need it more. This too can be done in a similar way to a laser, where a beam of liquid white light either washes or burns the disease away from the outside in, or from the inside out.

With these forms of Abstract Imagery, sometimes the disease, especially when it is cancer, will be seen to be cleared completely in a particular session. Other times, and for other people, it may seem that only partial progress is made. This can be fine as long as you (yourself) feel confident with the amount of progress in any given session, and that you avoid any temptation or tendency to worry. Ideally, to repeat, the aim is to do these exercises with a good feeling and plenty of confidence.

Please be aware that these Healing Imagery techniques and principles apply well to pain control. As this is another large area to consider and as it was well covered in my other books, if you are interested in this aspect, please do refer to Chapter Six in *You Can Conquer Cancer* (pages 70 to 83) and Chapter Ten in *Peace of Mind* (pages 177 to 180.)

A final note on Abstract Images. If you reflect on this for a moment, probably the most Abstract Imagery of all would be to use the simple silence of meditation. If you imagine clearly in your mind that when you enter the stillness of meditation, your immune system will be free to heal you powerfully and effectively, then by starting with this strong intention, and believing that you will be activating subtle but powerful Imagery forces; then you will in fact be using the most Abstract Imagery of all. It is my belief that when the two elements are combined in this way, Abstract Imagery with the stillness of silent meditation, then remarkable and profound healing becomes a strong possibility.

Having considered how to heal the body in some detail, now let us move on to consider how to heal the heart.

CHAPTER 14

HEALING THE HEART

Imagery's precious gift

Forgiveness, equanimity, loving kindness, compassion, joy. Getting to know yourself better. Making friends with yourself. Being able to give more love unconditionally. Simple warm-hearted kindness. Who could not do with more of these qualities of the heart in their life?

While we all may honour these attributes and hope to demonstrate them in our daily lives, how can we actively develop them? This is where Imagery has a major contribution to make in our personal development. With Imagery there are reliable techniques for fostering just these ideals. For those who are motivated, you can learn and practise Imagery exercises that will help you to forgive, that will generate loving kindness and compassion.

What follows are key techniques that I have used personally and have taught to others. Some of these techniques did in fact develop out of the needs of people in our groups. Some I learnt from other Teachers, most of them are taught by one of my own great teachers — the Tibetan Lama Sogyal Rinpoche.

For the fact is that while over the last few centuries, the Western world has been busy developing the Intellect and studying science, for thousands of years people in the East have been busy studying the mind and developing Wisdom. So most current psychotherapy practices can be traced back to origins in Eastern techniques. Buddhist practices particularly, are very rich in this area. You may well benefit, therefore, from referring to Sogyal Rinpoche's book, *The Tibetan Book of Living and Dying*, on those techniques also — especially his

Chapter Twelve on Compassion. What I have done here is to put in my own words those practices that I have found most beneficial. I do so offering respect to their original sources and the many people who have helped me to be able to explain them in what I hope will be a form that is easily accessible. (Having said that I would emphasize that another of Sogyal Rinpoche's many gifts is his ability to do just that — to translate ancient techniques into a form that is readily accessible for modern people.)

Addressing 'Healing the Heart' we will focus on four main practices:

1.   Getting to know our own true nature

2.   Compassion

3.   Forgiveness

4.   The traditional and profound practice of Tonglen

These practices will be presented in a structured way. Spending some time on each, in this particular order, will help to make each successive practice easier. Any one of these techniques could be used over a long period of time, and to develop them fully that is what is required for most people. In a practical sense, however, they do interact with each other — reinforcing, supporting and making each more accessible and possible. So for most people it works best to focus upon each technique, working through them one at a time and spending at least a few weeks on each. You are bound to notice that some of the techniques seem to offer you more than others. The best approach is to practise each technique for long enough (usually two to four weeks) to obtain a good *feel* for it. Then you will know what you need to do — whether it is time to move on to the next technique, or to spend longer on this particular one. Here then are these key Imagery practices.

1. Getting to know your true self

In our essence, we are whole and pure. In our essence — whole and pure. Do you know it? Do you believe it? Do you hope to experience it?

To experience this reality directly is the aim of deep spiritual practice. To experience our own true nature as being whole and pure, is to know our own true worth. And it is to know from direct experience the interconnectedness of all things. It is to know that at this deep level there is a common factor, a common ground that links us all.

With this knowledge, of our own innate goodness and of our interconnectedness, there comes a natural respect for self and for others. There comes too a capacity to recognize the sacred in all things, and the compassion to understand the inequities and sufferings around us. There is a natural urge to forgive our self and others, a natural urge to be kind to our self and to others, and a natural urge to live a life based upon compassion and loving kindness.

People learn to meditate for many reasons. Stress management, increased coping skills, healing illness, peace of mind. The greatest gift meditation offers is the possibility of a direct experience of who we really are, of our own true nature, our good heart. So learning to meditate is the greatest gift you can give your self.

And the essence of meditation is to be found in simple silence. When we let go of all our busyness, all our *doing*, and rest in our natural state of *being*, then our good heart is revealed, and we experience this essence directly.

This style of meditation, based upon simple silence was introduced to me at the start of my illness by the late Dr Ainslie Meares. His approach is well presented in two of his main books *Relief without Drugs*, and *The Wealth Within*. In a more traditional way Sogyal Rinpoche teaches the practice of Dzogchen, the highest form of Buddhist meditation practice. This is well described in *The Tibetan Book of Living and Dying*.

My own book *Meditation — Pure & Simple* focuses on techniques that can help you to relax physically, calm the mind and then move into the simple silence of profound meditation.

At the risk of over-repetition, I will say it again. Practising simple meditation provides a view and a foundation from which all else becomes more possible, more balanced and more effective. Therefore, I recommend this to be your core practice and that you spend some time each day letting go and being still. Certainly doing this will make the following practices more possible.

2.   Compassion

Sogyal Rinpoche values compassion so highly that he describes it as 'the wish fulfilling jewel.' In his words, to have compassion for another person

> *'is not simply a sense of sympathy or caring for the person suffering, not simply a warmth of heart toward the person before you, or a sharp clarity of recognition of their needs and pain, it is also a sustained and practical determination to do whatever is possible and necessary to alleviate their suffering.*
>
> *Compassion is not true compassion unless it is active.'*

Here are six wonderful Imagery exercises that progressively build compassion. Prepare for each one in the standard way to begin any practice. Attend to your outer environment, your attitude and then relax physically and calm your mind through the use of the Relaxation Response. Then you are ready to begin. Most people find these exercises easier with their eyes closed.

(a)   The Loving Kindness exercise

Imagine as if they were in front of you, the person who has loved you most in life. Traditionally your mother is recommended, but if that is not so easy, recall a person and a time when you felt deeply loved. Perhaps an image of that time comes with the image of the person. Most importantly recall the feeling, this person's unconditional positive regard for you (their love!), their acceptance, their warmth. Give yourself over to these feelings, the aim is to build the feeling of loving kindness as strongly and clearly as you can. As you feel that love rising within your heart, return the loving feeling to this precious person. Return the love almost as if you are radiating it back to them.

Now imagine a neutral person in your life as if they were standing beside the person who loved you most. This will be someone who you know quite casually, but who you know well enough to bring to mind clearly. As you imagine them in front of you, radiate those feelings of loving kindness to them. You may do this simply in a feeling sense, radiating the feeling to them and feeling it wrapping all around and through them, warming their heart and filling them with loving kindness. Many people find it helpful to visualize the loving kindness in the form of White Light, to see this Light well up in their own heart and then to radiate it out like a search light, a beam of light that travels to the other person's heart. There it fills their heart with the same clear White Light before radiating out and filling their entire body; perhaps even wrapping around them too like a cloak or blanket.

If you have difficulty with this, return to the person who loved you most; rekindle, rebuild the feelings of loving kindness and then radiate them to the neutral person. Keep doing this, moving from one to the other, until you feel the neutral person is as filled with loving kindness as the person who loved you most.

Now imagine a person who has been difficult in your life as if they are before you and repeat the exercise, sending the same feelings of loving kindness to them. If you have difficulty with this, return to the person who loved you the most, re-establish the feelings and then radiate them to the difficult person.

Keep alternating between the three people until the feelings for all three are the same. You may like to end by resting with the feelings of Loving Kindness, almost as if you are absorbed in those feelings.

(b)   Consider Your Self the Same as Others

The Dalai Lama says this so clearly:

'All human beings are the same — made of human flesh, bones and blood. We all want happiness and to avoid suffering. Further, we have an equal right to be happy. In other words, it is important to realize our sameness as human beings.'[1]

To contemplate this deeply, to realize that even the difficult people in our lives are just like us and are seeking the very same things that we are, is to open our heart, to provide insight and generate active compassion.

(c)   Walk in the Other's Shoes

In Buddhism this is called 'Exchanging yourself for others.' American Indians echo the same sentiment when they say 'Never criticize another before you have walked a mile in their moccasins.'

This is another key technique which I have found helpful for many people. So often we react to the difficult people in our lives with anger and disgust. This exercise has the potential to reframe our view by adding understanding and fostering compassion. Imagine the life of the other person. Where were they born, what were their parents like? What type of upbringing might they have had, what were their formative influences? What has been happening for them recently? What suffering have

---

1.   The Dalai Lama, *A Policy of Kindness*, (Ithaca, N.Y. *Snow Lion*, 1990 and quoted in *The Tibetan Book of Living and Dying*.)

they known? How did they get to the point in life they are at now?

Personally, it has been a very helpful exercise for me to contemplate, in this way, the lives of people who perpetrate crime and bring real suffering into the lives of others. It is an exercise I found revealing of myself and my previously ingrained attitudes, and one I have felt great benefit from. I recommend it highly.

(d) Using a Friend to Generate Compassion

This is something of a variation on the previous exercise. Instead of putting yourself in the other's shoes, you imagine a dear friend or loved one in their place. By imagining this person who is so precious to you, in the place of someone else who is suffering, you will open your heart and feel moved to be of direct help.

(e) Considering the Plight of Others

It is so easy to be confronted by suffering in this modern world. We travel so much, the media presents so much, communication is so easy and frequent. Many it seems, deal with this barrage of suffering by attempting to avoid it or by switching off all together. There is a deeply concerning trend that many adults, and especially so many children, are becoming desensitized to suffering. They do not want to acknowledge it, know it or understand it. It is too much to bear.

How then is it possible to open to the range of suffering around us and to not be overwhelmed? The answers to this crucial question lie in the personal practice of contemplation. Do take the time, make the time to reflect on the nature of suffering. As you recognize that everyone suffers in one form or another, just as you do your self, it will challenge you, confront you and it may well inspire you. You need to open to this, there comes a vulnerability with this type of contemplation. It can take you into deep and scary places. It can take you into the mystery of life. It can open profound compassion and this practice may well transform your life.

This practice particularly links into the traditional practice of Tonglen which we will investigate later in this Chapter.

(f)   How to Direct your Compassion

The use of the compassion exercises already described is bound to move you towards an even stronger, heartfelt desire to help others. This motivation, particularly when it is based upon the contemplation of suffering and compassion, is bound to have a pure intention. There are two ways to put this heartfelt desire into action.

The first is to fervently pray that all your actions will benefit others and bring them happiness. I felt that this prayer was an important part of my healing, I reaffirmed it every time that I meditated. Now it is the basis of the work I am involved in and I continually remember to come back to it and align my life with its intention in the best way I am able.

The second practice in Buddhism is called Bodhicitta. This means 'to awaken and develop the heart of the enlightened mind' and to dedicate any merit we may have to the benefit of others. We aim to reach our own enlightenment, so that we can be of more help to those around us, and we dedicate the merit of that enlightenment towards helping others to reach that same state.

By practising compassion, we become far more aware of the real needs of ourself and others. As a consequence, issues of Forgiveness often arise. In my experience, taking the time to actively generate compassion is often a prerequisite that helps to reveal the importance of forgiveness. Often too, it is the practice of simple meditation and deep compassion that can help to make possible the difficult task of true Forgiveness.

3. Forgiveness

Dawn was a dear friend who I had known for many years. When she was diagnosed with bowel cancer, it was already very advanced, there was no effective medical treatment for her. Dawn's condition deteriorated rapidly and I was with her the day she died.

Dawn had lived an extraordinary life. Having been committed to the spiritual path, she had met many great Masters as well as engaging in many personal development practices. As her body had weakened, her spirituality shone forth even more. So as she seemed so close to dying, I asked her if she was ready, if there was anything else she needed to do, and how I might help. There was little real response to this, so I sensed to ask her if there was anyone she needed to forgive. Dawn reflected for a few moments and said, 'Well yes, there is my father.'

Now I had known Dawn for many years and it struck me immediately — I had never heard her speak of her father. I asked her what she might need to forgive her father for. She replied, 'Well, he could have been there a bit more for me.' As we talked on, Dawn elaborated. Her father it seemed, had been a somewhat abusive drunk and her mother had left him when Dawn was only five years old. He had suffered a stroke several years later and died when Dawn was nine. When I asked her how she felt at that time, she said it made little difference for her in her mind, he was dead already!

Dawn went on to tell me that in fact her father had remarried and had another daughter before he died. I had known nothing of this half sister's existence and I suspected Dawn's only son did not know her either. To my amazement this actually was the case and I suggested Dawn may like to talk with her son about it all. She agreed and did so later.

What struck me most, however, was how Dawn had done so much personal development and spiritual practice, yet here she was, literally on her deathbed, still holding resentment for her father. I could not help but relate this to the many,

many relationships Dawn had entered into with men that had lasted a while, but then more often than not, in fairness, been fractured by Dawn's own initiative and behaviour.

It seemed easy to link the two. So here was Dawn, so close to death, her father still unforgiven. I asked her if she could forgive him now. 'Oh yes,' she said, 'that would be easy.' She sighed deeply, lay back, her whole demeanour relaxed and she slept deeply. After she awoke, Dawn spoke with her son and then died peacefully later in the day.

How extraordinary that it was only on her deathbed that Forgiveness became possible. And that then it was so easy and brought such great relief.

The moral? True Forgiveness is difficult. We need to be highly motivated to do it. Once done, however, Forgiveness brings a sense of relief and release and a deeply abiding inner peace. Forgiveness has played a key role in the healing of many people who have experienced remarkable recoveries. Forgiveness is a key to enduring health and wellbeing.

Why then is Forgiveness so hard? To understand this, often we need to begin by understanding what forgiveness is *not*. While it is nice to be positive, there are many misconceptions regarding Forgiveness, so to clarify what it is *not* helps to make Forgiveness more possible

Forgiveness is not saying it was OK. To forgive we need to acknowledge the wrong, the hurt, the injustice. Often we may need to seek reparation in the courts, to bring the offender to justice. We can acknowledge the suffering caused by the act, while forgiving the person.

Forgiveness is not saying it is OK for it to happen again. This is a key issue which often I find more of a problem for women than men. The myth is that if you forgive it will happen again. Forgiveness is clear in saying that it was not OK and that it is not to happen again. So frequently a big part of Forgiveness is establishing, or re-establishing personal boundaries. This involves being clear about what you will accept or put up with — and what you will not; and being strong enough in your self to maintain those boundaries.

Forgiveness is not forgetting. While in some situations it can be useful to forget the little hurts and slights and simply move on, we are talking about something different here. When Forgiveness is a major issue, attempts to forget are more likely to be forms of denial. Denial can help short term but it tends to lead to bottling of emotions with explosions at inopportune times. Forgiveness does not wipe the memory. It does however, let go of the pain attending that memory.

Forgiveness does not mean you have to be friends. Sometimes Forgiveness does clear the air and heals old wounds in a way that allows for the re-establishment of important relationships. This often happens with blood relatives. However, with other people it may well be different. This reveals a key underlying issue which explains why some people find it hard to forgive old partners. While you hang on to resentment, you hang on to the person to whom the resentment is attached. It may not be very pleasant, but you still have the hooks in. If you have put a huge emotional investment into this other person and hoped to get something back; if it has not worked out the way you had hoped and you continue to blame them, and hold them in resentment, there is always the outside chance that they may be shamed into realizing the errors of their ways, to relent, repent or in some other way give something back.

The challenge with true forgiveness is that it is unconditional. Forgiveness that says 'I will forgive you *if* …' or 'I will forgive you *when* …' is a start, but it is hollow. True Forgiveness has no conditions. You have to give it away. It is the same as unconditional love — a gift from the heart. When you have been deeply wronged, no wonder Forgiveness is so hard!

Forgiveness is not easy. The point of all this is that you really have to want to do it. It helps to experience the cost of ongoing resentment. The Buddhists say that being angry with another person is like picking up a hot coal and throwing it at your enemy in the hope of hurting them. At the very least you can be sure the act will hurt yourself, what it does to the other is somewhat in the lap of the Gods! Perhaps we need to suffer the pain of resentment long enough and deep enough before we are clear on the merit of practising Forgiveness. Then the work begins.

Preparation for Forgiveness

As with most of these key Imagery exercises, the preparation provides an essential platform or foundation which makes the main practice possible.

For Forgiveness, the ideal preparation includes simple meditation, compassion exercises and suffering! For most of us it is only when we see through the ongoing and deep suffering that resentment causes ourselves and others that we become ready to work on Forgiveness.

Then one of the key exercises that I do find helpful is unsticking some of the resentment glue, and allowing an opening to the possibility of Forgiveness, is the Compassion exercise of putting yourself in the other person's shoes. This can help you to understand and feel into what it was that caused the other person to act the way they did, to feel an empathy, a compassion that makes Forgiveness more possible.

The Practice of Forgiveness through Imagery and Affirmation

This exercise was first recorded in *You Can Conquer Cancer*, (pages 156–158) and is repeated here with some additions. You begin in the standard way, relaxing through the Relaxation Response.

Visualize the person you are considering. It can be satisfactory to just concentrate on them, but try to build up as clear an image of them in your mind as you can, as if they were sitting in front of you and you were looking directly at them. Some people find it helpful to begin by looking at a photograph, so fixing the person in their mind.

Then use these four phrases, repeating each one silently to yourself, over and over, until you can say it with conviction, before going on to the next:

> *I forgive you.*
> *Please forgive me.*
> *I thank you.*
> *I bless you.*

As you begin this exercise, you will find that it takes an effort to concentrate on the person's image *and* the repetition of 'I forgive you, I forgive you'. However, fairly soon you are likely to find yourself dwelling on all the good reasons why you should *not* forgive them.

'Forgive *them*! I have every reason to hate that person!' you may think. Every reason, except that the hate affects *you* more than anyone else! As you dwell on it more, a wider, healthier perspective will come.

As you keep repeating the phrase, you enter into meditating upon why you should forgive them. Think of all the reasons they are like they are, why they did what they did. You will find yourself slipping over into contemplation and a new insight developing. As you continue you *will* reach the point where, with conviction you can say, 'I forgive you!'

I found 'Please forgive me' was the hard one. While at first I was beset by all the reasons why I should not forgive this person, how horrible they had been, how much they had hurt me; as I persevered I came to realize my own role in all the problems. If I had behaved differently, the whole situation would have developed in a better, more harmonious way. The exercise led to remarkable insights and reframed my whole experience.

'I thank you' was usually a major test, too. Thanking someone for putting you through a hard time that finally taught you so much demands a perspective of Forgiveness and acceptance. This exercise develops a great understanding of life and relationships in general.

'I bless you' is easy after the first three have reached the point of conviction. It is a release, a letting go. At that point you recognize the worth in the other person. While you may agree to differ on points of view, you are now free to go your independent ways without any negative attachments.

I found it good to start this exercise with easy things, like the man who cut you off while driving home, the lady who stood on your toe, or the shop assistant who was so difficult. It is a good thing to do as a regular exercise, choosing one person a day for a while. I used to recall someone that I had met during each day and practise the exercise 'with' them. Soon I found the whole thing happening automatically as any incident occurred. If a difficulty with a relationship looked like developing, it was as if those four little phrases whizzed around in my head, defusing the situation even before it developed. Then I worked on the hard relationships, the cluttered old ones from times gone by. The effect was considerable. I really felt freed of old attachments.

Alcoholics Anonymous takes this idea further and suggests that reformed alcoholics should make restitution to people they have harmed. They recommend actually fronting such people, apologizing and doing all they can to physically make good any loss they caused. I do not think it is necessary to go that far unless you want to. However, I know it works, for there was one particular person whom I had been involved with in a difficult way and had not felt comfortable with since. I practised this technique until I really could genuinely say those four statements. When I then called on the person, the atmosphere between us was totally different to the usual tension. We fell easily into an extended talk, discussing all our old problems, and both left feeling lighter and happier. It amazed me that the whole nature of that relationship was balanced by that exercise. Many of the people in our groups have found it works for them and I recommend this exercise in Forgiveness highly.

4. Tonglen

This is perhaps the most important of all these exercises in the potential benefits it offers. This too can be a difficult exercise to begin; it can reveal many hidden apprehensions, fears and false views you may have been conditioned into holding. However, it offers a vehicle for major inner work, major inner transformation and the prospect of more fully realizing your true nature.

Tonglen is a practice that involves giving and receiving in a way that you may not have thought of previously. It is not uncommon for people to recoil from it a little at first, before deep reflection reveals its merits.

In Tonglen, the aim is to take in all the difficulties of others and to give out your own good qualities. This is done in association with the breath. You breathe in the pain and suffering of others, and breathing out, send them your own inner peace, happiness and welling.

By taking in the suffering of others, especially when that suffering takes the form of emotional pain or physical disease, many people are concerned that they might distress themselves, or worse, make themselves sick. What experience demonstrates, is that the practice does confront these issues, does challenge that ego-based part of our being, does confront our fears. However, very directly it does help us to rise above all that so that we can experience a stronger and more profound level of compassion. This leads you to be able to practise Tonglen even more effectively, with more conviction and impact.

If you choose to practise Tonglen, I strongly recommend you study *The Tibetan Book of Living and Dying* on pages 201–208 so that you benefit from Sogyal Rinpoche's tradition and experience with this technique. While Tonglen is a Buddhist practice, it is eminently suitable for everyone and I can recommend it highly.

Sogyal Rinpoche recommends that to begin the practice of Tonglen you do it with yourself first. This will help you to learn the technique, to adjust inwardly to the practice, and then to be able to practise it with other people. While I have used these practices extensively myself and taught them to others, please acknowledge that I am drawing heavily on Rinpoche's very clear instructions.

Preparing for the Practice of Tonglen

Begin in the usual way, as for meditation, and then aim to still your mind as completely as possible. As you allow your thoughts to settle, as you let go and enter into this deeper stillness, you begin to rest in 'the true heart of the enlightened mind.' When you feel ready, begin the practice.

The Preliminary Exercises of Tonglen

Environmental Tonglen

Be aware of your own state of mind. Notice whatever is moody, dark, angry, frustrated; whatever emotions we normally describe as negative. Breathe these qualities in on the in-breath, then breathe out the 'positive' emotions — peace, calm, clarity, joy. Repeat this until you feel the atmosphere around you, the environment, to be cleansed.

Self Tonglen

This time, as you breathe in, draw in all those aspects of your self that you are unhappy about. Imagine breathing in all your own hurts, resentments, negativities, injustices. Now, imagine that all that is good within you receives this suffering. That all that is good and life-affirming within you, accepts this pain, and really feels it all. In response, your good heart is opened, your good heart embraces the suffering, absorbs the suffering. In turn, in response to this, all the negativity melts away and these two aspects merge into a mental feeling of compassion and loving kindness.

Tonglen in Life

Imagine a situation in life that has left you feeling shamed or guilty. As you breathe in, accept responsibility for what you did, without any attempt to rationalize or justify your behaviour. Earnestly ask for Forgiveness. Breathe out Forgiveness, healing and understanding. This exercise can reinforce, even add another dimension to the Forgiveness exercise. It is certainly made easier if you have done the latter already, and the two exercises complement each other well.

Tonglen for others

This is like the exercise in Loving Kindness, only this time after you imagine someone who is very close to you, you breathe in their pain and suffering. Breathing out, you send them your own inner peace, love, healing, joy. You then repeat this with the neutral person and the difficult people in your life.

These are the preliminary practices. By spending time on each one, you will become familiar with the technique and the benefits, and be both inspired and ready to utilize the main practice.

The Main Practice of Tonglen

1. The preparation. Relax through the Relaxation Response, let go of thoughts, allow your mind to settle. Then deeply contemplate the nature of Compassion, using whichever method works best for you to arouse the strongest feelings of Compassion that you can. Invoke the presence of the embodiment of your own truth — whether it be the presence of God, Christ, the Buddha or the more abstract presence of Universal Love and Energy.

2. Imagine as if they were in front of you, someone who you care for and who you know is suffering. As you feel your compassion go out to this person, imagine all their problems and difficulties, all their suffering as if it is a cloud of hot, black, grimy smoke or vapour.

3. Now imagine that all your own negativity is like a band or barrier around your own heart. As you breathe in,

draw in the black smoke and imagine that it is drawn into that band of negativity around your heart. As it does this it causes all your negativity to dissolve.

4. Imagine that as your negative barrier is dissolved, your own good heart shines forth. This heart is full of radiant, clear White Light. As you breathe out, you release this radiant light, carrying with it all that is life affirming — peace, joy and happiness. The outbreath carries this light with it to your loved one and it purifies their negativity on every level. This flow of compassion carries with it the fervent wish to alleviate the suffering of the other person.

    By breathing in you absorb the suffering of the other person, this transforms your own suffering, releasing your finest qualities which you breathe back to the other. So while your motive is to help the other person, the dual effect is to transform your own inner being.

5. As the light of your heart and compassion touches the other person, feel a deep joy that they have been freed of their pain and suffering. Continue with the practice, breathing in their suffering, breathing out your own healing, love and compassion.

This exercise can then be done with any other person. It is an excellent exercise if you want to help someone in need of healing, or someone who may be close to dying. Also, it can transform the way you feel and interact with difficult people in your life. It is a *wonder-full* practice. Again in Sogyal Rinpoche's words:

> 'This holy secret of the practice of Tonglen is one that the mystic masters and saints of every tradition know; and living it and embodying it, with the abandon and fervour of true wisdom and true compassion, is what fills their lives with joy.'

CHAPTER 15

IMAGERY AND TRUTH

What are you really seeking?

Recently, in a fairly large workshop, I was leading the participants through the series of meditative experiments that so often lead into stillness. These exercises are detailed in *Meditation — Pure & Simple* and begin by simply observing the thoughts. The intention is to notice how your thoughts form — that in fact they form as images made up of pictures, sounds (often words in the form of an inner dialogue) and feelings. Then we notice how each thought is like a segment or unit, with a beginning, a middle and an end point. Next we notice the gap between one thought ending and the next beginning. Of course, in this gap between two thoughts is a moment of silence. So noticing the gap can lead us into this silence.

Through direct experience it is possible to realize that this silence is the sacred ground out of which all things arise and into which all things settle. This is in Truth, God's territory.

Very often the images in our mind, the images that come to mind, can be instrumental in leading us into the direct and profound spiritual experience of simple silence.

Having completed the exercises at the workshop, one of the men shared his experience. His eyes were alight, he was sitting forward, almost half standing in the way of someone filled with joyful enthusiasm. His face was radiant as he described what had happened. He had begun to notice his thoughts fairly visually when a new image automatically came to mind. He recalled the toy train of his early childhood. The train had little wooden carriages held together with simple metal links. Now the carriages seemed to represent and carry his thoughts, the links felt as if they were the obvious gaps between the thoughts. As he focussed on the gaps, he focussed on the metal links. These links then proceeded to dissolve. The sense was that as the links dissolved, the carriages followed and soon all that was left was a large fog in front of his eyes.

With a huge smile this man described how he felt that he had a lot of courage to enter into this fog. Then as he spoke on, his gaze went inwardly to some distant place, the way people often do when they touch something profound. He said when he was young he had read and remembered a beautiful quote *'All is one, one is all.'* He remembered thinking when he first heard it how nice it was; it had touched him deeply, and he had hoped that he might come to know it for truth.

With his face beaming, amidst a flurry of awkward giggles and smiles, he said how he had passed through the fog to a state where that oneness was revealed to him by direct experience. Having said this, he could say no more. He was mildly overwhelmed, mildly ecstatic. Deeply joyful. Radiant.

So as we come to the end of this work — a summary, some encouragement and some final suggestions.

Imagery is to do with the mind. Imagery is the language of the mind. Imagery is the tool of the mind. The mind is extraordinarily powerful. The mind is a double-edged sword — it can be powerfully destructive, powerfully creative.

For many of us the conditioning of past experiences, the conditioning stored in our memory as images, limits the capacities of our mind. For many of us, to actively work on reprogramming the mind is, therefore, a key step in freeing us from past limitations and opening us to future possibilities.

However, if we limit ourselves to what the mind alone is capable of, we limit ourselves to what can be rationalized, analysed, broken into smaller pieces or built up with methodical planning. While this may well have its benefits, clearly it has its limitations. For the truth of the matter is that the essence of life, the heart of life, is essentially mysterious.

Love, Hope, Faith, all that we really value, all that has true substance; all these mysteries dwell in the realm beyond the thinking mind.

Once again, then we return to the need for balance. Yes, it makes sense, profound sense to rationally address the workings of the mind; to understand the key role of Images and Imagery in our lives and to use this understanding with more awareness, with more good effect.

And clearly too, for completeness and for the opportunity of finding what we are really looking for, we need to go beyond the mind, perhaps using Imagery as the vehicle to transport us beyond the thinking mind, into the magical stillness of our own true essence!

BIBLIOGRAPHY

Clynes, M., *Sentics — The Touch of Emotions*, Garden City, New York, Anchor Press Doubleday, 1978.

Dossey, L., *Healing Words*, San Francisco, Harper Collins 1993.

Frankl, V., *Man's Search for Meaning*, New York, Pocket Books, 1963.

Gawler, Ian, *You Can Conquer Cancer*, Melbourne, Hill of Content, 1984.

Gawler, Ian, *Peace of Mind*, Melbourne, Hill of Content, 1987.

Gawler, Ian, *Meditation — Pure & Simple*, Melbourne, Hill of Content, 1996.

Krystal, P., *Cutting the Ties That Bind*, Maine, Samuel Weiser, Inc. 1993

Maltz, M., *Psycho-Cybernetics*, Sydney, Bantam, 1978.

Meares, A., *Relief Without Drugs: The Self-Management of Tension, Anxiety and Pain*, London, Collins/Fontana, 1970.

Meares, A., *The Wealth Within*, Melbourne, Hill of Content, 1978.

Simonton, O.C., *Getting Well Again*, Sydney, Bantam, 1978.

Sogyal Rinpoche, *The Tibetan Book of Living & Dying*, London, Rider, 1992.19

The Australian Concise Oxford Dictionary, Melbourne Oxford University Press, 1987.

The Holy Bible, Revised Standard Edition, New York, Thomas Nelson, 1972.